MADAME BOVARY

The End of Romance

TWAYNE'S MASTERWORK STUDIES
ROBERT LECKER, GENERAL EDITOR

MADAME BOVARY

The End of Romance

ERIC GANS

Twayne Publishers • Boston
A Division of G. K. Hall & Co.

Madame Bovary: The End of Romance
Eric Gans

Twayne's Masterwork Studies No. 23

Copyright © 1989 by G. K. Hall & Co.
All rights reserved.
Published by Twayne Publishers
A division of G. K. Hall & Co.
70 Lincoln Street, Boston, Massachusetts 02111

Copyediting supervised by Barbara Sutton.
Book Production by Janet Zietowski.
Typeset in 10/14 Sabon with Horley Oldstyle display type
by Compset, Inc. of Beverly, Massachusetts

Printed on permanent/durable acid-free paper
and bound in the United States of America.

Library of Congress Cataloging-in-Publication Data

Gans, Eric Lawrence, 1941–
    Madame Bovary : the end of romance / Eric Gans.
        p.   cm.—(Twayne's masterwork studies ; no. 23)
    Bibliography: p.
    Includes index.
    ISBN 0-8057-7984-1.   ISBN 0-8057-8033-5 (pbk.)
    1. Flaubert, Gustave, 1821–1880. Madame Bovary. I. Title.
    II. Series.
PQ2246.M3G25   1989
843'.8—dc19   88-24155
                                                           CIP

Contents

Note on the References
and Acknowledgments

The text of *Madame Bovary* used for this work is the Classiques Garnier (Paris: Editions Garnier, 1957, 1971). Citations are to part and chapter of the novel. Quotations from the correspondence are from Jean Bruneau's edition in the Bibliothèque de la Pléïade (Paris: Gallimard, 1973, 1980). All translations in this volume are my own.

The frontispiece photograph of Gustave Flaubert is reproduced through the courtesy of the Archives Photographiques, Caisse Nationale des Monuments Historiques, Paris, the S.P.A.D.E.M., and A.R.S., their representative in the United States.

Gustave Flaubert. Courtesy of the Archives Photographiques, Caisse
Nationale des Monuments Historiques, Paris, the S.P.A.D.E.M., and A.R.S.,
their representative in the United States.

Chronology:
Gustave Flaubert's Life and Works

1821   12 December, birth in Rouen of Gustave Flaubert, second son of Achille-Cléophas Flaubert, medical director of the city's main hospital, and his wife, Anne-Justine-Caroline, née Fleuriot. The father is a self-made professional, son of a veterinarian from the Champagne region; the mother, an orphan of the local gentry. Gustave's brother Achille, who will follow in his father's professional footsteps, is nearly nine years old.

1824   15 July, birth of Gustave's sister, Caroline. Gustave became very attached to her; after she died of childbed fever at age twenty-two, he remained devoted to her daughter (also named Caroline) until his own death.

1832   Composes plays to be acted out on his father's billiard table with Caroline and friend Ernest Chevalier.

1834–1835   Flaubert, in *cinquième* (seventh grade) at the Collège Royal de Rouen, produces his first literary efforts, including a "literary journal" entitled *Art and Progress*. One of his first extant works is a dance scene that is the far-off ancestor of the Vaubyessard ball in *Madame Bovary*.

1836   Summer, meets Elisa Schlésinger, a married woman some ten years his senior, for whom he will maintain a long quasi-Platonic attachment. This "great love" inspired the figure of Mme Arnoux in his *Sentimental Education* (1869).

1837   February–March, with the help of his friend Alfred le Poittevin, Flaubert has two of his short stories published in a Rouen literary magazine, *Le Colibri*.

1838   Composes *Mémoires d'un fou (Memoirs of a Madman)*, in which he recounts a romanticized version of his meeting with Mme Schlésinger.

1840   August, receives his Baccalauréat (high school diploma).

1841–1843	Pursues law studies in Paris with no great enthusiasm or success.
1842	Composition of *November*, an autobiographical work inspired by youthful experiences of love and sexuality.
1843	February, begins his first novel, *Sentimental Education* (not to be confused with the rather different novel published under this title in 1869).
1844	January, a severe epileptic attack both forces and permits Flaubert to abandon his legal studies, and with them, all thought of an active career. For the rest of his life he will devote himself entirely to his writing. Jean-Paul Sartre (*The Family Idiot*) considers this attack the decisive event of Flaubert's life.
1845	January, completes *Sentimental Education*. Perhaps as a result of the crisis of January 1844, the novel changes sharply in tone in the later chapters, which emphasize the life of the artist Jules over the worldly Henri whose adventures had dominated the first part.
1846	January–March, deaths of Flaubert's father and sister Caroline; lives with his mother in Croisset (a suburb of Rouen) until her death in 1872. June, meets Louise Colet, with whom he will maintain a stormy relationship until 1854; many of his most important letters are addressed to her. August, writes to Louise Colet: ". . . what I love above all is form, provided it be beautiful, and nothing else. Women whose hearts are too ardent and whose minds are too exclusive don't understand this religion of beauty detached from feelings."
1849	September, completes the first version of *The Temptation of Saint Anthony*, which his friends Louis Bouilhet and Maxime du Camp urge him not to publish. A month later, he leaves with du Camp for two years of travel through the Near East, Greece, and Italy.
1851	19 September, begins *Madame Bovary*.
1852	January, writes to Louise Colet. ". . . what I would like to write is a book about nothing. . . . The most beautiful works are those in which there is the least matter. . . . I think the future of Art lies in this direction. . . . Form, in becoming dexterous, is attenuated. . . . That is why there are neither beautiful nor ugly subjects, and one might almost establish as an axiom that, from the point of view of pure Art, there are no subjects at all, style being all by itself an absolute way of seeing things." March–May, composition of chapters on Emma's

childhood, the Vaubyessard ball. July, completes draft of part 1 of the novel; attends an agricultural fair in preparation for the *Comices Agricoles* in part 2. September–October, composition of the opening scenes of part 2, including Emma's romantic conversation with Léon.

1853   June, writes to Louise Colet: "I now feel for my fellow man a serene hatred, or a pity so inactive that it's just the same. . . . The political state of affairs [Napoleon III's authoritarian regime] has confirmed my old *a priori* theories about the featherless biped [man], whom I consider to be at the same time a turkey and a vulture." July–December, works on the Agricultural Fair scene. August, writes to Louise Colet: "Everything we invent is true, be sure of that. Poetry is as precise a thing as geometry. . . . My poor Bovary, no doubt, is suffering and weeping in twenty French villages at once, at this very moment." December, works on Emma's seduction by Rodolphe. Writes to Louise Colet: "Today . . . man and woman together, lover and mistress all at once, I rode on horseback in the forest . . . and I was the horses, the leaves, the wind, the words they said to each other and the red sun that half-closed their eyelids drowned in love."

1854   May, makes final break with Louise Colet. The termination of their correspondence makes it difficult to follow the composition of the remainder of *Madame Bovary*.

1855   May, begins work on part 3 of *Madame Bovary*. September, writes to Louis Bouilhet: "I hope that within a month la Bovary will have her arsenic in her belly."

1856   April, completion of *Madame Bovary*. May, correction of the final copy. The chapter divisions within the three parts were added at this stage. October, writes to Mme Roger des Genettes: "People think I'm in love with reality, but I despise it. For it was out of hatred for realism that I undertook this novel." October–December, installment publication of *Madame Bovary* in the *Revue de Paris*.

1857   January–February, Flaubert, together with the director and printer of the *Revue de Paris,* is tried for "offenses to public morality and religion" in publishing *Madame Bovary*. He is acquitted along with his codefendants. March, writes to Mlle Leroyer de Chantepie: "There is nothing true in *Madame Bovary*. It's a *totally invented* story; I put nothing in it of my feelings or of my existence. The illusion (if there is one) comes on the contrary from the *impersonality* of the work. . . . The artist should be in his work like God in creation, invisible and all-powerful; one should feel him everywhere, but one should not see him." April, publication of *Madame Bovary* in book form by Michel Lévi. Flaubert would always regret having sold Lévi his five-year rights to the novel for the modest sum of 800 francs. (About $8,000 today, if one considers that the book—in two volumes—sold for two francs.) September, begins work on his next novel, *Salammbô*.

1858   April–June, trip to North Africa to do research for *Salammbô*, which is set in ancient Carthage (now Tunis).

1862   November, publication of *Salammbô*.

1864   September, begins work on his most ambitious novel, *Sentimental Education*, a historical transformation of the first (1845) version in which the protagonist's romantic illusions are coordinated with the failure of the Revolution of 1848.

1869   November, publication of *Sentimental Education*, a few months before the Prussian victory over France puts an end to the Second Empire of Louis-Napoleon Bonaparte. Flaubert, disappointed with the relative lack of interest in his novel, would claim that if the French had read it attentively the disastrous war of 1870 might have been averted.

1872   April, death of Flaubert's mother; retains habitation rights at Croisset, ownership of which passes to his niece.

1872–1873   Having completed the final, greatly reduced version of the *Temptation of Saint Anthony* (June 1872), Flaubert tries his hand at the theater, with little success. He also begins his last novel, *Bouvard and Pécuchet*, at which he will work until his death.

1874   April, publication of *The Temptation of Saint Anthony*.

1875   Financial ruin to Ernest Commanville, the husband of his niece Caroline. Flaubert sacrifices his financial security to protect the young couple.

1875–1877   Composition and publication of the *Three Tales (A Simple Heart, Saint Julian the Hospitaler,* and *Hérodias).* In these stories, as opposed to the novels, the protagonists attain a form of religious salvation analogous to that of the extra-worldly artist. Flaubert returns to work on *Bouvard and Pécuchet*.

1879   In financial straits, accepts a government sinecure of 3,000 francs per year.

1880   May 8, dies from a stroke at his home in Croisset. *Bouvard and Pécuchet,* nearly complete at the time of his death, is published the following year. A few months after Flaubert's death, his niece sells the Croisset property; the house is torn down and a distillery built on the site.

1

Historical Context

French cultural life at the time when Flaubert was writing *Madame Bovary* was dominated by the disillusionment with romantic cultural and political ideas that had followed the events of 1848–52.

In February 1848 the monarchy of Louis-Philippe, itself founded in 1830 on the overthrow of the Restoration monarchy, was overturned and an abortive Second Republic created. Flaubert, often thought of as a political reactionary because of his artist's contempt for the masses, reacted positively to the February revolution. The revolt was led by men of the same social class as his father, the so-called capacities or professionals who felt underrepresented in Louis-Philippe's regime, which favored financial and landowning interests.

The choice of the poet Lamartine as the first leader of the new regime was a clear sign of the connection between romantic culture and romantic politics, a link stronger and more apparent in France than elsewhere. By the same token, the death of the Second Republic after a mere three years with Louis-Napoleon Bonaparte's December 1851 coup d'état was a demonstration of the bankruptcy of romantic ideals. After dissolving the Republic's ineffective parliament, Louis-Napoleon had his action confirmed by plebiscite, and became France's second emperor a year later. He ruled France until 1870, when his regime was brought down by its disastrous defeat in the Franco–Prussian war.

The events of 1848–52 taught the bourgeoisie a lesson that Karl Marx for one would make much of: that it was no longer a revolutionary class but a conservative one. This change became visible as early as June 1848 in the young republic's crushing of a worker's rebellion. Romanticism had held forth the perspective of universal harmony through the pursuit of the revolutionary egalitarianism of 1789; the "days of June" made it clear that the old division between the "Third Estate" and the privileged aristocracy was no longer the hot point of social conflict. Henceforth the middle classes were threatened not from above but from below, and whether they accepted this fact or not, only an authoritarian regime of the sort that Louis-Napoleon provided was fitted to deal with this problem. By electing him in December 1848 by a huge majority as the first (and only) president of the Second Republic, the French citizenry was in effect asking for the coup d'état that he would carry out three years later.

The Second Empire was for the French bourgeoisie, to which its most important writers and artists belonged in spite of themselves, a period more of humiliation than of actual suffering. The coup d'état had demonstrated the political, but not the economic, bankruptcy of this class. The bourgeoisie had proved unable to govern France, but once relieved of the burden of government it prospered more than ever. Industrialization began in earnest during this period. Paris was redesigned in more or less its present form; for reasons of military security, the wide boulevards we know today were sliced through the crowded neighborhoods of the old city, affording huge opportunities for real estate speculation and construction.

Although Napoleon would mellow in the 1860s, the early years of the Second Empire during which *Madame Bovary* was written were repressive and alienating. Flaubert, who would later frequent the imperial court, had no love for the emperor, but the brutal extinction of the hapless Second Republic confirmed his intuition of the self-indulgent mendacity of romanticism, both in art and in politics.

While some, like Victor Hugo, who remained in exile from France for the duration of Louis-Napoleon's regime, never lost faith in the romantic ideal, the most characteristic cultural achievements of this period reflected a drastic reassessment of the artist's role. For the romantics, the artist's intuition of personal uniqueness was the fundamental source of aesthetic originality; the generation of the 1850s distrusted the personal and sought to expel it from their works. Inspired by the great popular painter Gustave Courbet, a "realist" school of novelists emerged in this period, emphasizing the less glamorous aspects of life that had been neglected by the romantics. The only product of this group still remembered by nonspecialists is Henri Mürger's *Scenes of Bohemian Life,* which later inspired Puccini's opera *La Bohème.* This sentimental depiction of the lives of struggling young writers and artists hardly corresponds to what we would call "realism" today. Flaubert had no relations with these writers, who signally failed to realize that *Madame Bovary* represented the real fulfillment of their doctrines. Yet two of the best novels of the school, Champfleury's *The Bourgeois of Molinchart* and Duranty's *The Troubles of Henriette Gérard,* which describes the difficulties of a strong-willed young woman who could almost be taken for a heroine of George Eliot, have a good deal in common with Flaubert's masterpiece.

Charles Baudelaire's *Les Fleurs du mal* (*The Flowers of Evil*), perhaps the most significant book of poetry ever written in France, appeared in 1857, the same year as *Madame Bovary.* Only a few months after Flaubert had been acquitted of the charge of offending "public morality and religion," Baudelaire was convicted of the same offense, obliged to pay a fine, and ordered to remove six "obscene" poems from his book. In sharp contrast to the romantic poetry that Hugo was continuing to write, Baudelaire's poems were short, with an emphasis on fixed forms (most are sonnets), and took a blatantly theatrical, ironic attitude toward the truths of personal experience. Baudelaire was the first to understand the problematic, guilty nature of the poetic self who dares to write the word "I." The romantics had fancied themselves the universal spokesmen of humanity; Baudelaire emphasized the poet's necessarily hateful egoism. Woman in Baudelaire's poetry is not an object of male protection; both angel and monster, she is man's dangerous Other, and ultimately his double. *Madame Bovary* would demonstrate woman's central role in modern society; Baudelaire displayed the bitter ironies inherent in affirming at all cost the poetic self's masculine perspective.

Although Baudelaire's influence would be supreme among the poets of the following generation, in England as well as in France, the dominant poetic school in Flaubert's time was that of the "Parnassians," whose name was derived from that of a widely read anthology, *Le Parnasse contemporain.* The Parnassians emphasized the precise, impersonal description of stark natural scenes as well as "noble" classical and religious subjects. Leconte de Lisle, the leading figure of this school, heaped scorn on the romantics for their shameless baring of their souls in their poetry. Flaubert sympathized with Leconte's lofty aims, but found his work too idealized and the man himself a bit of a prig.

It may safety be said that without the events of 1848–52 Flaubert would never have written *Madame Bovary.* Like many latecomers to romanticism, the young Flaubert was unable to operate effectively within its limits. His first novel, the 1845 version of *Sentimental Education,* had lost its concrete focus on the worldly hero Henri as the author turned to a contemplative analysis of the budding literary career of the "artist" figure Jules. Flaubert seemed incapable of taking a middle path between depiction of the vanity of worldly desires in a satiric and ultimately indifferent tone and subjective identification with a character who was little more than a mouthpiece of the author. Nor does the 1849 version of *The Temptation of Saint Anthony* provide a genuine solution to the problem of constructing a unified literary work. The saint is tempted by figures of sins, heresies, and monsters of all sorts; these fascinate him, but he can neither conquer nor succumb to them. The self, as modeled by Anthony, is divided between a worldly part that must be rejected and a spiritual part that has no real content of its own. Only the failure of the romantic political experiment could provide Flaubert with the humiliated self that would create a new form of novel.

His innovation was this: the author would no longer identify with the characters, inhabiting their world in the form of a personal narrator, but must remain apart from it and them. The truth about human society could only be observed from without, not lived from within. No reconciliation was conceivable between worldly and authentic existence; but the author could forget about attempting to reconcile them, and the world would nonetheless continue to exist. Emma Bovary, Flaubert's heroine, would demonstrate the vanity of any such attempt; the author, detached from his fictional universe, would neither share nor condemn her illusions.

The acceptance of a separation of the world of the novel from the author's own consciousness, perpetuating the split that romanticism had promised to repair, was the beginning of a new cultural era that would lead in the century that followed *Madame Bovary* to increasingly radical experiments in an art of alienation. The most extreme of Flaubert's successors would speak of literary language as an autonomous force independent of the imaginary world it depicted. The artificiality of the literary would be continually emphasized, and the reader's presumably naive attempt to deal with the fictional world as though it were a real one would be systematically frustrated.

In the minds of the radical moderns, the last vestiges of the romantic ideal of harmony between the imagination and the real were being purged; yet this ideal always sprung up again, if only to be purged anew. Flaubert and Baudelaire had fewer illusions about the process they had set in motion. The appearance in 1857 of *Madame Bovary* and *Les Fleurs du mal,* two sister works conceived out of the frustration of the bourgeois idealism of 1848, marks the birth of aesthetic modernism as the never-ending transcendence of romantic illusion.

2

The Importance of the Work

Madame Bovary marks a watershed in the history of the novel. No serious novelist writing after 1857 could ignore its standard of stylistic and formal perfection, and the influence of its subject was felt throughout European literature. Tolstoy's *Anna Karenina* (1877) and the German novelist Theodor Fontane's *Effi Briest* (1895) are the two most striking attempts to create variations on the theme of the unsatisfied married woman: even the women's names seem to pay homage to Flaubert's heroine.

Madame Bovary owed much of its early success to the scandal of the trial in which its author was finally acquitted of the charge of offending "public morality." But even before the trial, when the novel was not yet available in book form, it had become a cause célèbre. Flaubert's first readers sensed that the novel as they knew it had undergone a major transformation in both content and form, that personalized narration based on a common experience of life had been replaced by the systematic observation of a milieu with which the author refused to identify. Flaubert's choice of a protagonist of the opposite sex is a revealing sign of this refusal of identification; the novel would henceforth be the story not of a surrogate self but of an Other. The reader's chief point of contact with her is not personal but *cul-*

tural; the determining factors of Emma's inner life are the romantic dreams she has obtained from books. By refusing either to endorse or to condemn these dreams, the author suggests that within the world no truer perspective is available. *Madame Bovary* is a study in the futility and the necessity of worldly desire.

Several new narrative techniques give form to this vision. Flaubert was not the first novelist to describe the world of the novel largely from the point of view of his main character, but he was the first to refuse to counterbalance this subjective material with the observations of an objective narrator. Flaubert innovated the extensive use of *free indirect discourse,* a form previously used almost exclusively for the reporting of speech, to present his heroine's desires as an integral part of the narrative. Flaubert's narration breaks with the traditional opposition between event and background: imperfects ("he was going") are blended with normal past tenses to create "typical" scenes that seem both to be uniquely taking place at a given moment and to be repeated an indefinite number of times. Finally, Flaubert's *phenomenological* style deliberately rejected the harmonious rationality of French prose by breaking sentences into small fragments and subverting their natural rhythm; the form of Flaubert's language continually undercuts the significance of its content.

The extreme meticulousness of the composition of this novel, which took its author more than four years to write, its documentation of points of technical detail, and above all its merciless unmasking of romantic illusions made it the first work to justify the idea, still revolutionary in its time, that the novel was truly the major art form of the modern era. Since the Renaissance, the drama had been the most prestigious and universal genre because the characters' confrontations are told in their own words rather than being transmitted by a historically bound narrative voice that always risks becoming archaic. The technique of *Madame Bovary* makes it the first novel to justifiably make this same claim of universality. The author's refusal to infuse his narrative with the ethical attitudes of his time allows successive generations of readers to judge Emma and her world on their own merits.

That *Madame Bovary* is the story of a middle-class woman's frustrations is not original in itself. But Flaubert alone understood the significance of this theme to be not the exposition of the wrongs inflicted on women by bourgeois society, but the revelation of the "feminine" nature of the modern self, of its Otherness. Emma is not a symbol of oppressed womanhood, but a model of the human condition. The secondhand quality of her dreams of love and luxury, narrated in the impersonal mode of free indirect discourse, makes her a forerunner of the men and women of the consumer society that was only to come into full-fledged existence with the rise of mass production and the mass media after the first World War. Her subjectivity, both naively open to influence and hermetically closed upon itself, remains a provocative model for our own.

Although Flaubert's technique of impersonal narration would make him the precursor of the most radical currents of the experimental novel in our century, his writing does not represent, as some of his recent admirers have claimed, a radical break with the traditional narrative. *Madame Bovary* is not a book in which language operates on its own without the help of a clear plot and well-defined characters. Nor is it the "novel about nothing" that Flaubert said he wanted someday to write. Emma is a representative of Otherness, not nothingness. Yet in its subtle subversion of the author–reader relationship, *Madame Bovary* has had a more radical effect on the form of the novel than earlier works like Diderot's *Jacques le fataliste* or Sterne's *Tristram Shandy* that had gone to far greater lengths to undermine the illusionary basis of narrative fiction. By dissolving the unspoken sense of community that links reader and narrator as human beings who understand the world in essentially the same way, Flaubert paved the way for the more radical separation between writing and storytelling carried out by his successors in the twentieth century.

But Flaubert never abandons the storyteller's concern to maintain the reader's interest in his tale. We may not be able to define the voice that is the source of Flaubert's narrative, but we are never in doubt as to what is taking place. We may be shown at every turn that Emma's desires are nothing but copies implanted in her by the religious and literary discourses she has absorbed, but we never cease to be concerned with them. For if Emma's illusions are those of an Other, they are never subjected to the easy mockery of the author-as-Self. Emma captures our imagination because our imagination, as Flaubert understood far better than his avant-garde disciples, is the principal faculty of our own Otherness.

Flaubert was the first writer to accept this shared otherness as his only possible point of contact with the reader. But the traditional clarity of his narration is not a relic of the past that would mark him as a transitional premodern figure. It is a sign of his understanding that the modern era, however much he affected to despise it, was continuous with the past. Flaubert rejected the romantic illusion of immediate communion, but not the human need for communication. *Madame Bovary* is both modern and timeless because its author was able to fashion the contradictions of the dawning modern era into a timeless model of the human predicament.

3

Critical Reception

Madame Bovary was never Flaubert's favorite among his works. Throughout the period of its composition, he complained of the mediocrity of his characters and their world, yearning, like his heroine, for a stage more worthy of his performance. No letter in his correspondence triumphantly announces the conclusion of the manuscript. When he writes to Louis Bouilhet on 1 June 1856 that he has sent off the novel to the *Revue de Paris,* he is already immersed in a revision of *The Temptation of Saint Anthony* and in preparations for *Saint Julian the Hospitaler* (which he would finally write only in 1875). On 5 October, on seeing the first published installment of *Madame Bovary,* he writes to Bouilhet: "The sight of my work in print has put me in a stupor. It struck me as altogether dull. I can't see anything in it."

Yet this novel, the realization of one of the most scrupulously conceived of all literary undertakings, is deservedly the principal source of its author's fame. Few works of the modern age have received more critical attention than *Madame Bovary,* and even fewer have remained so consistently in the limelight from the time of their publication. Its installment publication in 1856 in the *Revue de Paris* brought it to the attention of literary circles; the publicity of the trial early in the following year made it a best-seller. It has since remained the most widely read of all French novels, both in France and around the world.

Critics were at first divided between admiration for the novel's indubitable craftsmanship and originality, and shock at the new impersonality of its tone. The more moralistic readers (including the prosecution at the trial) were not altogether off the mark in detecting in Flaubert's narrative a nihilism subversive of socially accepted ethical values. The tone of this sort of criticism was one of scandal rather than analysis. One critic called *Madame Bovary* "a poison which, disdainful of the poetry of vice, has taken only its brutality"; another said he could not analyze the novel because "art ceases when it is invaded by filth."

The most influential critic of the time, the scholarly, feline Sainte-Beuve, contributed greatly to the book's reputation with a long article that appeared in the official government journal *Le Moniteur* in May 1857, three months after the author's acquittal. Sainte-Beuve, who often heaped flowery praise on mediocre works and denigrated original ones, was openly appreciative of Flaubert's achievement, a judgment for which he was taken to task by a number of his less influential but more prudish contemporaries. Sainte-Beuve admired *Madame Bovary* for the "scientific" precision of its observations; while reproaching its author for "harshness," he saw the novel as typical of a generation that had rid itself of romantic illusions. His last sentence, which both describes this generation and alludes to Flaubert's father's profession, has become famous: "Physiologists and anatomists, I find you everywhere!"

Paradoxically enough, *Le Réalisme,* the journal of the realist school with which Flaubert would be associated despite himself, criticized the novel for representing "obstinacy in description" and lacking life or feeling: "This book is a literary application of the calculus of probabilities." No doubt Edmond Duranty, the author of these lines and a novelist in his own right, was not anxious to share the slogan of "realism" with a more powerful writer. The reproach of "mathematical" coldness is the understandable reaction of a group of writers whose choice of humble subjects did not preclude emotional identification with their characters. The realists were incapable of appreciating a narrative technique that liquidated the romantic sensibility that lingered on in their own works.

Although it was not particularly influential at the time, the most interesting early critique of the novel was that of Flaubert's greatest contemporary, the poet Charles Baudelaire. Baudelaire understood through his artist's intuition an aspect of the novel that later critics have grasped through readings of memoirs and letters: that *Madame Bovary* was a tour de force and that the banality of its subject matter had attracted Flaubert as a challenge. Baudelaire recognized the problematic identification (as opposed to straightforward narrative empathy) between the author and his heroine. His article emphasizes Emma's "masculine" nature, the strength of will she derives from her creator, the sense in which she too is an "artist" who creates her life out of her desires rather than passively accepting the split between desire and reality.

Despite its controversial beginnings, *Madame Bovary* was soon securely enshrined in the literary pantheon. The readers of the following generation were no longer shocked by Flaubert's "cruelty" to his heroine or by his "amorality," if only because, in large measure as a result of his influence, authorial distance had since become the norm. On the contrary, the pre-Flaubertian narrator's haste to supply the reader with a moral perspective on the characters' experience came to be felt as an inappropriate meddling with the reader's freedom of judgment.

In the French literary world, Emile Zola's *The Naturalist Novelists* (1881) named Flaubert as the greatest recent precursor of his own "scientific" school of Naturalism. For Zola, Flaubert's sober and scrupulous depiction of the details of everyday life made him the worthy successor of Balzac. Techniques like *typical narration* and use of free indirect discourse, while not discussed as such in Zola's critical works, became the staple of his own narrative art and that of his disciples. Guy de Maupassant, the nephew of Flaubert's childhood friend Alfred le Poittevin and for a time a member of Zola's school, memorialized

Flaubert's principles of composition in the preface to his novel *Pierre et Jean* (1888), emphasizing the precision of the master's technique of description.

Jules de Gaultier's work of aesthetic philosophy *Le Bovarysme* (1902), an expansion of an essay published ten years earlier, gave Emma Bovary's name to a vision of the human condition which consists in "thinking oneself other than one is." Although Gaultier condemns the excesses that lead to the destruction of persons like Emma, he considers "Bovarysm" to be "the principle of all progress" and the basis of human freedom. Gaultier's book demonstrates that by the turn of the century *Madame Bovary* was recognized in France as the privileged expression, in both its positive and negative aspects, of the alienation—the Otherness—of the modern self.

Flaubert's influence was also felt in the English-speaking world. The influential British essayist Walter Pater (1839–94) wrote admiringly of the principles of artistic detachment that Flaubert expressed in his correspondence, and that he put into practice in *Madame Bovary*. Henry James, an even more significant figure, was deeply influenced by Flaubert's impersonal narrative mode. A great admirer of *Madame Bovary*, James nevertheless found the cast of petit-bourgeois characters repellent, and was unable to generate any enthusiasm for the later novels. James's novelistic practice makes it clear why he could give only partial adherence to his predecessor's doctrine. James's abandonment of the narrative function to his characters is indeed very different from Flaubert's; it relies on their profundity, whereas Flaubert refuses to attribute to his characters any profundity whatsoever. A later British critic, Percy Lubbock, whose influential *The Craft of Fiction* (1921) is still widely read, was less guarded in his enthusiasm; for Lubbock, *Madame Bovary* "remains perpetually the novel of all novels," the touchstone against which all novelists after Flaubert were forced to measure themselves.

Marcel Proust, the author of the 3,000-page *In Search of Lost Time* (best known in English under the unfortunately inaccurate title *Remembrance of Things Past*), also expressed admiration for Flaubert in a celebrated article written in 1920 to defend him against a journalistic attack on the purity of his style. Proust was the first to comment on the aspects of Flaubert's style that I have referred to here as *typical narration* and the *phenomenological* sentence structure. For him, these qualities of "grammatical beauty" were perhaps inferior to the wealth of language to be found in more spontaneous artists, but they were all the more to be admired as products of painstaking creation. In expressing these sentiments, Proust, who does not appear to have been familiar with Flaubert's *Correspondence,* was no doubt unaware how close they were to Flaubert's own. In a letter written to Louise Colet during the composition of *Madame Bovary,* Flaubert had drawn this same distinction between the great natural artists and those, like himself (and Louise), whose art required unceasing self-discipline.

Flaubert's hostility to the egalitarian political movements of his time brought him under attack from the socially committed, "engaged" writers of the 1930s and 1940s. Jean-Paul Sartre, whose obsession with Flaubert would later inspire the huge three-volume literary-biographical study *The Family Idiot* (1971–72), dismissed him as an unwitting bourgeois apologist in his *What Is Literature?* (1948). The great Hungarian Marxist critic, Gyorgy Lukacs, who had admired Flaubert in his early writings (*Theory of the Novel,* 1920), condemned him from the 1930s on as a "decadent" in comparison to the true realism of Balzac. Lukacs's hostility to Flaubert may strike non-Marxists as dogmatic, but he was more acutely aware of Flaubert's aesthetic contempt for worldly action than those who naively praised or condemned his "realism." In Flaubert's model of bourgeois society, the class struggle sacred to Marxists is but another romantic illusion.

The instant notoriety and enduring popularity of *Madame Bovary* have been of interest in their own right to critics bent on understanding the contradictory self-consciousness of modernity. Sartre made the popularity of this antibourgeois novel among the bourgeoisie of its time the privileged subject of the "internal–external" analysis described in the "Search for a Method" (1956); this essay later became the opening section of his *Critique of Dialectical Reason* (1961). (A fourth volume of *The Family Idiot* was to have been devoted to a detailed analysis of *Madame Bovary;* a posthumous publication is currently in preparation.) Hans-Robert Jauss, the founder of the influential German school of "the aesthetics of reception," chose the same example in his well-known 1970 essay "Literary History as a Challenge to Literary Theory." Jauss compares the success of *Madame Bovary* in 1857 with the even greater success of the now-forgotten *Fanny* by Ernest Feydeau, a far more sexually explicit tale of adultery. He explains the indictment of Flaubert's rather than Feydeau's novel for immorality on the grounds that the impersonality of free indirect discourse denied the reader's moral views their expected foothold in the world of the novel.

Traditional criticism, friendly or hostile, emphasized the realistic aspect of Flaubert's creation. The new attitudes toward the novel that emerged in the postwar years have put their emphasis rather on Flaubert's "de-realizing" side. French "new novelists" like Nathalie Sarraute and Alain Robbe-Grillet saw Flaubert as a precursor of their attempts to undermine the expectations generated in the reader by traditional narration. Their novels, whose "unreliable narrators" are radically estranged from the reader's common experience, are the often disconcerting products of a radical application of Flaubert's doctrine of authorial impersonality. The similarity of the new novelists' aims to those Flaubert had expressed in his correspondence was brought to the attention of the intellectual and scholarly community in Geneviève Bollème's widely read *The Lesson of Flaubert* (1964).

Still more recently, Flaubert has been a great favorite of poststructuralist criticism; a 1986 volume entitled *Flaubert and Post-Modernism* attests to this continuing interest. Among the more stimulating studies of the deconstructionist school, Jonathan Culler's brilliantly tendentious *Flaubert* (1974) attempts to show how the author's "uncertain" narrative voice draws the reader unsuspectingly into a meaningless world. A subtle recent analysis by Michal Ginsburg, *Flaubert Writing* (1986), analyzes *Madame Bovary* and the other novels as the work of a Beckett–like author whose characters are means of continually regenerating a narrative always in danger of petering out.

Scholarly studies and readings of Flaubert's works continue to appear in ever-increasing numbers. The French school of *genetic* criticism pores over Flaubert's voluminous plans and drafts in its attempt to reconstruct the stages of composition of his novels. Students of *narratology* investigate the linguistic and semiotic aspects of Flaubert's narrative technique. Feminists provide new perspectives on Emma's plight; Marxists interpret the impersonal language that surrounds her as the reflection of a new stage of capitalist evolution.

While other writers drift in and out of fashion according to the fluctuations of critical taste, Flaubert remains the one French writer of his century that no theoretician of literature can ignore or disparage. It would be difficult to name a major literary critic since the publication of *Madame Bovary* who has not written on Flaubert. This is more true than ever today.

Flaubert's other novels are much admired and specialists can make a case for preferring the author's own favorite, *Sentimental Education*. But both in the world of academic criticism and scholarship and among the general public, *Madame Bovary* has never lost its leading position in Flaubert's oeuvre. It remains today, as it was already in 1857, the one uncontested masterpiece of the French novel, and one of the great literary accomplishments of all time.

A Reading

4

Flaubert before *Madame Bovary*

Gustave Flaubert was born on 12 December 1821 in Rouen, the me-
tropolis of Normandy. He was the second child of Achille-Cléophas
Flaubert, the chief physician of the Hôtel-Dieu (main hospital) of
Rouen, and his wife, Caroline. Achille-Cléophas was an ambitious
man from the Champagne region, the son of a veterinarian. His medical career was a distinguished one, but it lacked the ultimate fulfillment of an appointment in Paris. Gustave's mother was an orphan of
genteel Norman stock whose mother had belonged to the minor nobility. She was a sensitive woman, a frequent sufferer from migraine
headaches.

Gustave was one of only three children; several other siblings died
in infancy. As a child, Gustave was overshadowed by his brother
Achille, nine years his senior, who would eventually follow in his father's footsteps as Rouen's chief surgeon. Like a number of romantic
writers (Byron, Chateaubriand, Balzac), Gustave was very close to his
sister, Caroline, three years younger than he. Her death shortly after
childbirth in March 1846 (two months after the death of their father)
left a great void in his emotional life, which was only partially filled
by his attachment to her daughter, also named Caroline, whom he and
his mother brought up.

From an early age, literature became an outlet for Gustave's frustrations. In his first letters, dating from the age of ten, he writes to his friend Ernest Chevalier about the plays he, Ernest, and Caroline performed on his father's billiard table. Although these plays have been lost, a large collection of school "creative writing" assignments and other youthful compositions remain. In these early works, Gustave adapts romantic narrative and occasionally dramatic forms to the working out of his family conflicts. Writing has already become his chief source of self-satisfaction, both through the creation of revengeful scenes of wish-fulfillment and, more significantly, through the pathetic dramatization of the hero-victim's fate. The unhappy central figure suffers the cruelty of successful "brothers" and indifferent "fathers" and is consoled at times by compassionate "mothers."

In "Two Coffins for an Outlaw," the fourteen-year-old Gustave's version of Prosper Mérimée's "Mateo Falcone," where a father kills his son to save the family's honor, Gustave has the mother, unlike the submissive figure of the original, commit suicide (whence the "two coffins") to protest her son's death. Several of these early stories feature a female protagonist. In "Les Baladins" (*baladins* are itinerant street performers), Marguerite, the unattractive heroine, loses her husband to a beautiful rival and ends her sufferings by a suicide that already bears some resemblance to Emma Bovary's. In an epilogue to this story, the fifteen-year-old author exults in the writer's power to dominate the world of his creation, a power illustrated in many of his early writings by a sado-masochistic insistence on the sufferings of characters with whom the author explicitly identifies.

"Passion et vertu" (Passion and Virtue), written at the age of sixteen, is the juvenile work that most closely anticipates *Madame Bovary*. It is the story of Mazza Willers, a passionate, unhappily married woman who, abandoned by her lover, commits suicide by taking arsenic. The tale is told in a romantic mode foreign to the mature novel, but the resemblance in both the plot line and the personality of the heroine is undeniable. The young writer already found feminine desire—the desire of the Other from a masculine standpoint—of greater interest than the more aggressive masculine variety. Mazza, who kills her husband and children as well as herself, is a far more active figure than Emma would ever be, but the essence of her position remains passive: the love she desires cannot be sought directly, but must come to her from without. Thus she sacrifices all for her lover, but cannot seek satisfaction on her own; Emma will suffer a similar fate.

Although Gustave's literary activity had absorbed his interest since childhood, it would have been unthinkable for the son of a self-made professional like Dr. Flaubert to consider writing as a career. Achille, the elder brother, was the father's chosen successor in the medical profession, so after completing his studies at the Rouen *lycée*, Gustave set off for Paris in 1840 to study law. But Gustave detested his legal studies, at which he was not very assiduous. In 1843 he began work on his first full-length novel, entitled *L'Éducation sentimentale (Sentimental Education)* which shares with the mature novel of the same title (1869) the theme of a young man's progression through romantic illusions of love to the sterility of disillusionment. Gustave nevertheless continued to prepare himself for a legal career, until he was saved from it by an incident that Jean-Paul Sartre recognized as the central event in establishing his career as a writer.

In January 1844, while returning home to Rouen with his brother Achille after inspecting a new family villa on the seacoast, Gustave was stricken with a mysterious attack that modern medical opinion has diagnosed as a form of epileptic seizure. He remained in a weakened condition for several months, and as a result took on within the family the status of a semi-invalid unable to pursue a professional career. Gustave abandoned his legal studies and devoted himself to literary activity on a full-time basis.

After the deaths of his father and sister in 1846, Gustave, who never married, remained at home with his emotionally dependent mother until her death in 1872. They were charged with the care of sister Caroline's infant daughter, whose father became insane after his wife's death. For the remainder of his life, Flaubert would reside in the family property at Croisset, a village near Rouen, voraciously reading the works of classical and modern authors and working on his novels and other literary projects. The legend of the "hermit of Croisset" is, however, inaccurate. Aside from trips to the Near East, North Africa, and England, Flaubert maintained throughout most of his adult life an apartment in Paris where he spent a good part of the winter months.

Flaubert also led an active and varied sexual life, although he had few real love affairs, with none serious enough to make him consider marriage or even cohabitation. His stormy liaison with Louise Colet, which lasted from 1846 to 1854, is chiefly of interest to us for the two hundred-odd letters Flaubert wrote her; a cynical reader gets the impression that this was its chief interest for Flaubert as well. The recent discovery of a long-standing affair with Juliet Herbert, one of his niece's English governesses, who made a first, unfortunately lost, translation of *Madame Bovary*, adds a spiritual note that is lacking almost everywhere else in the tale of Flaubert's love life.

The first literary result of the crisis of 1844 was the sharp new turn given to *Sentimental Education*. What had begun as the story of the disillusionment of the worldly Henri tailed off into a series of reflections on the life of the contemplative Jules, who decided to consecrate his future to Art. The novel as completed in 1845 lacks unity, as Flaubert himself recognized, and was never published in his lifetime. But this very disunity is the sign that the author could no longer be satisfied with the romantic identification between protagonist and narrator that had characterized his earlier fiction. A gap had opened up between art and life, desire and aesthetic creation, that would furnish the creative tension from which his mature works would emerge.

Three years later, in 1848, while France was in the throes of the series of revolutionary events that would put an end to romantic illusions in the political sphere, Flaubert began *La Tentation de Saint Antoine* (*The Temptation of Saint Anthony*). As long as a full-length novel, the *Temptation* follows the format of romantic "philosophical drama," written to be read, not performed. The saint's temptations include the Seven Deadly Sins, all manner of heresies and philosophical positions, and a lengthy series of gods, idols and monsters. This work draws its interest from a never-stated analogy between the saint's need both to experience and to resist the visions of desire and the condition of the writer-artist confronted with the worldly materials of his creation. But in this first version, in contrast with the far shorter and more sober work eventually published by Flaubert in 1874, Saint Anthony is unable either fully to accept or to reject the necessity for his temptations. The last lines show the saint in prayer as the sun rises, putting an end to his nocturnal fantasies, while the mocking voice of the Devil threatens him with further trials to come. This conclusion is quite different from that of the 1874 version, where Anthony goes beyond the question of grace or damnation to achieve spiritual peace in a pantheistic union with protoplasmic matter. Anthony's wish is no longer to possess his visions as objects of worldly desire, but to assume their fallen, "stupid" material being as his own. The solution to the temptations that plagued the saint in the first version is the dissolution of the barrier between Self and Other. This is the aesthetic attitude that would dominate the works of Flaubert's later life.

Over a period of three evenings in the fall of 1849, Gustave read his massive opus to his friends Louis Bouilhet and Maxime du Camp. Appalled by the work's lyric excesses, and perhaps unfairly indifferent to its merits, they pronounced on the *Temptation* a verdict of utter condemnation. Gustave should "burn his manuscript and never speak of it again"; in the future, he should treat a subject taken from everyday life, like the later novels of Balzac. The blow was a harsh one, but in retrospect beneficial to Flaubert's literary career. After a twenty-month trip with Maxime through the Middle East, Greece, and Italy (1849–51), during which the modernistic du Camp took the first photographs of the Egyptian pyramids, Flaubert returned to Croisset determined to get to work on a new project. This project was *Madame Bovary*.

5

Madame Bovary:
The Story

The plot of *Madame Bovary* can be told in a few lines. Charles Bovary, a recently widowed medical officer (a second-class doctor) in Tôtes, a small town in Normandy, marries a young woman he has met in the course of his rounds. Emma is a farm girl but she has been educated in a convent in Rouen and has acquired refined tastes. At first she experiences her marriage as a liberation, but she soon finds life with Charles, who is good-natured and affectionate but dull and unsophisticated, unbearably tedious. When the couple attend a ball given by a member of the local nobility, Emma sees a glimpse of a better life and loses patience with her marriage.

Emma's discontent leads the couple to move to the somewhat larger village of Yonville-l'Abbaye, where Emma, much to her chagrin, gives birth to a daughter. She becomes romantically interested in Léon Dupuis, a young law student, but the relationship never goes beyond the platonic, and Léon eventually leaves for Paris to pursue his studies. Emma then encounters the more worldly Rodolphe Boulanger, who becomes her first lover. She plans to run away with him, but he escapes her clutches by going off on his own. This rejection throws her into a deep depression. During her convalescence Emma turns for a time to the consolations of religion and plays theatrically at sainthood.

The Story

At an opera performance in Rouen, Emma runs into Léon, recently returned from his studies in Paris. Soon they too become lovers; this time it is Emma who takes the dominant role. But her extravagance has led the Bovary household into bankruptcy. Desperate to ward off the seizure of the family belongings, Emma is refused assistance by her local admirers and finally by her former lover Rodolphe. Realizing that she will never find the ideal love she seeks, and ashamed to face her husband's forgiveness for her excesses, she commits suicide by swallowing a handful of arsenic. Charles is disconsolate; crushed by his subsequent discovery of Emma's love letters, he dies shortly afterward, and their daughter is sent to work in a mill.

The only subplot of any importance is the success story of Homais, the local pharmacist, who befriends the Bovarys out of fear that his own illicit medical activities might be discovered. A memorably caricatural incarnation of the bombastic anticlerical French bourgeois, Homais is given to long pseudoscientific discourses. Homais is not without practical intelligence, but his shameless self-importance makes him the chief representative in the novel of what Flaubert called *la bêtise*, by which he meant rather "foolishness" than "stupidity." The essence of *bêtise* is faith in the omnipotence of worldly language, which takes the form of "received ideas" or clichés; these are never in short supply in Homais's tirades.

The last words of the novel tell of Homais's receiving a long-coveted government decoration. The pharmacist's success reflects the triumph of mediocrity in the world, and provides a kind of post factum justification for Emma's suicide.

Madame Bovary is divided into three parts of unequal length. This division was made in the early plans for the novel, whereas the chapter separations within the parts were only made on the final manuscript. The first part (about one fifth of the novel) ends with the young couple's move to Yonville, where the main action is to take place. The second, occupying nearly half the book, takes Emma through her first love affair up to the renewal of her relationship with Léon. The last part occupies about a third of the novel, from Emma's affair with Léon to her and Charles's deaths and Homais's decoration. One could therefore label the parts "Charles," "Rodolphe," and

"Léon"; Emma's life is divided among the three men on whom she pins her hopes for fulfillment.

Each part contains a major scene that marks a turning point in the heroine's life. In the first part, the Vaubyessard ball gives Emma a glimpse of the life-style of the nobility and brings to a head her disillusionment with her marriage. In the second, the Agricultural Fair scene (*les Comices Agricoles*), the most original in the novel from a technical standpoint, juxtaposes with savage irony the romantic clichés cynically employed by Rodolphe in his seduction of Emma and the bourgeois platitudes mouthed by government representatives at the fair. The third part contains a notorious scene in which Léon and Emma consummate their relationship in a cab driven through the streets of Rouen; in a daring narrative innovation, Flaubert describes the scene entirely from outside the cab.

ORIGINS AND SOURCES
OF *MADAME BOVARY*

The moment at which Flaubert decided to write *Madame Bovary* remains a matter of dispute among scholars. Maxime du Camp's memoirs, our chief source in this matter, were written long after the event and tend to be colored by their author's desire to show himself as the major influence in Flaubert's literary career. New evidence has nevertheless vindicated du Camp's claim that his suggestion of the "Delamare affair" was the germ from which the novel sprung. Flaubert had remained undecided throughout his Near Eastern voyage concerning the nature of his new project. A letter written to Bouilhet during the trip (dated 14 November 1850) shows him hesitating among three different conceptions: "A Night of Don Juan," which he seemed at first to favor, an Eastern tale about a woman in love with the god Anubis, and a novel about a mystical Flemish girl who dies a virgin. Critics have enjoyed speculating on the degree to which Emma's romantic religiosity finds it origin in this third project, which in fact resembles Zola's *Le Rêve (The Dream)* far more than Flaubert's novel.

The "Delamare affair" took place in the village of Ry, some thirty miles from Rouen. A young medical officer, Eugène Delamare, a widower like Charles Bovary in the novel, married a young woman named Delphine Couturier who shortly thereafter scandalized the area's inhabitants with her adulterous love affairs and extravagant spending. She died within a few years, apparently of disease rather than suicide; her husband, ruined and despondent, shortly followed her to the grave. Du Camp revealed this source in his memoirs published in 1882, two years after Flaubert's death; the name of Ry surfaced in an 1890 article in a Rouen newspaper by a writer more directly familiar with local history. This revelation provoked some credulous early critics to interrogate the habitants of Ry, several of whom were glad to furnish copious and highly imaginative accounts of village life that curiously resembled the details of Flaubert's plot. But although the general layout of Yonville-l'Abbaye, where the action of *Madame Bovary* takes place, bears a clear resemblance to that of Ry, sober scholars now conclude that the "Delamare affair" gave Flaubert no more than the starting point of his plot. As we have seen, the theme of the unsatisfiable nature of feminine desire had already preoccupied him in his youth; both in name and in character, Mazza, the heroine of "Passion and Virtue," bears a far more profound resemblance to Emma Bovary than does the unfortunate Delphine Delamare.

A number of other sources have been found for various aspects of Emma's life, ranging from a biography of the free-living wife of the sculptor Pradier (which Flaubert appears to have commissioned from her maid) to the author's own experiences with the passionate poetess Louise Colet. But however many details Flaubert may have gleaned from these sources about young women's dreams of love and luxury, they provide little insight into his creative process. What was crucial for the genesis of *Madame Bovary* was the coming together of three elements: the author's demonstrated fascination with the subject of woman's desire, the Delamare affair that gave his intuition a guarantee in ordinary reality, and his awareness that his literary aims would only be achieved through the disciplinary choice of this "mediocre" subject.

FLAUBERT'S METHOD
OF COMPOSITION

One of *Madame Bovary*'s most durably influential features has been its extraordinary craftsmanship. Writers since Flaubert's day have been inspired by the rigorous perfectionism with which he approached every aspect of the novel's composition, from the details of plot and characterization to the agonizing purification of his style. One important contributing factor to this interest has been the author's voluminous correspondence, the first portions of which appeared in 1884 (and which is only now appearing in an unexpurgated version). In a series of letters to Louise Colet and other literary friends, Flaubert gives day-by-day descriptions of the painful effort that went into the composition of various scenes of the novel, and expresses in uncompromising terms the lofty literary ideals he was attempting to carry out.

Foremost among Flaubert's aesthetic notions is the necessity for the artist to remain detached from the world of his creation, to avoid distorting its truth by his own desire. What has been called the doctrine of "art for art's sake" (*l'art pour l'art*) derives essentially from this single premise, with its important corollary that the work of art should be unconcerned with satisfying practical worldly ends of any kind. The artist should neither seek fame and fortune by appealing to the prejudices of his audience nor attempt to modify these prejudices by the use of social or political propaganda.

Flaubert's correspondence reveals a clearly postromantic combination of obsession with and detachment from the act of literary creation. Honoré de Balzac (1799–1850), the prolific author of *The Human Comedy*, so believed in the independent existence of his characters that on his deathbed he is said to have called for Bianchon, the doctor who appears in many of his novels. In contrast, Flaubert's characters are at once distanced objects of authorial manipulation and so much a part of him that his identity is lost in theirs. While working on Emma's suicide scene he writes with sadistic relish that "la Bovary" would soon have her arsenic in her belly, but he later revealed that on writing this scene he felt the taste of arsenic in his own mouth. The world of Flaubert's creation is alien to him, but precisely because he cannot relate to his characters as friends, he can only understand them through an involuntary, visceral identification. Flaubert was the first writer for whom normal human relations could no longer serve as a model of his relationship with his fictional universe.

Flaubert worked on *Madame Bovary* from September 1851 to April 1856, only interrupting his labors for occasional brief stays in Paris and, until 1854, even briefer meetings with Louise Colet. Flaubert kept all his manuscripts; the dossier of *Madame Bovary* includes dozens of plot outlines or "scenarios" and thousands of pages of drafts, many but by no means all of which have been published. Each scene was carefully planned in advance to fit into the overall plot, then composed and mercilessly corrected. Each sentence was read aloud in Flaubert's study or in his garden, in an alley he called his *gueuloir* or shouting-place; days were spent eliminating repetition of words and phrases within the same or succeeding pages. The drafts of most chapters are far longer than the final versions; in the later stages of composition, Flaubert eliminated whole scenes that he perceived as divergent from the main line of the novel.

There is more than a grain of truth in the often repeated idea that writing *Madame Bovary* was a disciplinary action, the result of a "punishment" inflicted on Flaubert by his friends after their condemnation of the lavishly romantic *Temptation*. Just as the highly controlled style of *Madame Bovary* contrasted with the lyricism of the earlier book, so was its banal setting an antidote to the *Temptation*'s fantastic exoticism. But the portrait of Flaubert as a natural romantic converted to realism by force understates his realization, expressed implicitly in his earliest works and explicitly in the first *Sentimental Education,* that the literary work must be cut off from the author's worldly self.

The *Temptation* had not in fact been a romantic exercise in self-indulgence, but an attempt to externalize the fantasies of the author's desire not as dashing heroes and lovely heroines but as the monsters of Saint Anthony's imagination. In *Madame Bovary* this distancing would find the concrete locus in human experience that had been lacking in the previous work. The novel's fantasies would not be attributed to a half-legendary third-century saint, but to a contemporary personage better known to the author, yet still more distant from him: a woman. *Madame Bovary* offers the first modern answer to the question that Sigmund Freud would ask in frustration seven decades later: "What does a woman want?"

6

The Theme: What Does
the Other Want?

Freud asked his famous question in a letter written late in his career
to Marie Bonaparte, a descendant of Napoleon and one of his most
prominent female disciples. Freud's frustration has been taken by
modern feminists as a sign of the male-centered nature of his doctrines
concerning human sexuality. Flaubert was no feminist either. The
clearest expression of his ideas about the relations between the sexes
is the following passage from his letter of 27 March 1853 to Louise
Colet: "Woman is a product of man. *God created the female, and man
created woman* [emphasis by Flaubert]; she is the result of civilization,
an artificial creation." Flaubert thus chose as the protagonist of his
first major novel the figure that the male writer had "created" in the
image of his own desire. Because woman is man's Other, we may justifiably rewrite Freud's question as: "What does the Other want?"
Madame Bovary puts the desire of this "artificial" Other at the center
of its model of human reality.

   This theme does not lack a history. In the High Middle Ages,
sexual love replaced universal brotherly love as the most accessible
model of the individual soul's relationship with God. But beyond the
exaltation and sublimation of desire exemplified by Dante's idealiza-

tion of Beatrice lies Freud's question. I desire the Other, but what does the Other desire? The question can never be altogether avoided, because as human beings, the Self and the Other are not essentially different.

Of the older works of French literature that take up this question, the most notable is Racine's *Phèdre* (1677), the masterpiece of French classical tragedy. For Racine, the heroine's desire is a monstrous craving for a return to darkness, a rejection of the light of civilized reason. The horror of this vision is the implication that man, unable to attain true selfhood on his own, is henceforth dependent on woman's desire. The beginnings of bourgeois society have undermined the self's traditional security. This was already apparent in the work of Shakespeare a century earlier; but it was Racine who associated man's weakness with the dominance of the feminine. The era of the heroic Self had given way to the age of the Other.

Flaubert's contribution to the understanding of woman's desire corresponds to a more advanced phase of social evolution than the preindustrial seventeenth century. For Flaubert, the Other's desire is as monstrous as for Racine; but the horror lies not in its regression to forbidden depths, but in its utter superficiality. Because Emma's desires are merely picture-book images, they can never truly be incarnated in the real world. Emma forever appears to skim along the surface of her existence, experiencing the concrete realities of her life in terms of the unrealistic imagery of romantic novels. Flaubert's conscientious attempt to understand Emma leads him to create a character monstrous in her very understandability. Emma never speaks an original word; not merely her conversations but her innermost feelings are taken from books—those she has read, but more significantly, those Flaubert himself had read and written.

The ultimate interest of the Other's desire is that it serves as a model for all desire, including that of the Self. In *Phèdre,* the young hero listens horrified as his stepmother's confession of love for him provides him with an identity he had been unable to find for himself. The same is true in the more banal world of *Madame Bovary.* Flaubert creates in Emma a model of all desire. The reader remains fascinated by her because he—or she—is placed in the position of filling the monstrous gulf in Emma's life between desire and fulfillment. Emma's at times feverish activity always has a passive basis; she desires to be desired. In the strength of this desire, we are forced to see the weakness of our own.

Emma inspires in us the same kind of frustration as a girl who dreams of being loved by a movie star. We can laugh at the naïveté of her yearning, but those who are not movie stars cannot help but feel humiliated by it. And what is most humiliating is that we desire despite ourselves to *be* that mythical movie star who would satisfy her. This analogy is, however, imperfect. In today's media-centered world, movie stars do exist, whereas Emma's ideal lover is a fictional hero whom no real human being could hope to emulate. For Flaubert, desire is inevitably the attempt to apply to the real world a set of culturally transmitted illusions. Far from being an intimate secret of the individual, it is knowable only through hearsay, through imitation and repetition, like the language of advertising.

No one knows whether Flaubert really said "Madame Bovary, c'est moi!" ("Madame Bovary is me!"), but the phrase remains memorable because it expresses the paradox of the male writer's identification with his female protagonist. In his review of *Madame Bovary*, Baudelaire remarked astutely on the "masculine" personality that revealed Emma's hidden identity with her creator. From her wedding night, when Charles rather than Emma "seemed to have been the bride," through her dominant role in the liaison with Léon, to her last encounter with Rodolphe where she tells him reproachfully what she would have done in his place, Emma gravitates toward a masculine role. Even in the course of her ostensibly submissive love affair with Rodolphe, she does not accept his attentions passively but drives him to more violent and compromising acts, forcing him to flee Yonville rather than go along with her plan that they run off together. Emma only agrees to play the woman's role on the condition that the man conform to a predetermined image of the romantic hero, a requirement no real man can fulfill.

It would be a distortion of Flaubert's achievement to understand

Emma's frustration in simplistically sociological terms as that of an energetic woman in an age that severely limited women's opportunities for creative activity. The aggressive, emasculating component of woman's desire was already present in *Phèdre*, where the heroine rewrites the story of Theseus' descent into the labyrinth to give herself the principal role, abandoning in the process Theseus' original mission of killing the monster-Minotaur. Emma's refusal to accept her lot in life is similarly subversive of the differences affirmed by bourgeois society. It demonstrates that henceforth the only desire with any potency is that of the Other; in the modern world, only the woman can be "masculine."

The supposedly inner-directed male Self imagines woman to be the independent, autonomous being he can no longer hope to become. Flaubert does not share the illusion of the Other's autonomy; Emma is no more self-determined than Charles or Léon. But in a masculine culture no longer able to take its own desire seriously, Emma alone still believes enough in its illusions to become a desiring subject. This Other-as-subject cannot be known through the empathy of shared experience. Emma is only accessible to the reader through the second-hand fictions in which her desires were first defined. But this combination of opacity and accessibility is that of human relations in general in a social order where an obsessive search for personal uniqueness expresses itself in forms taken from the repertory of mass communications.

7

"Impersonality": The Author
Replaces the Narrator

One of Flaubert's most famous aesthetic pronouncements was that "the author, in his work, should be like God in the universe: present everywhere, and nowhere visible" (letter to Louise Colet, 9 December 1852). Flaubert rejects the authorial role of writers like Balzac and Stendhal who talk to their reader like storytellers recounting their tales to a group of friends. His opposition between the author's "presence" and his "visibility" turns the familiar distinction between "showing" and "telling" into a fundamental principle of literary ethics. The author should *show* us the world of his creation, not *tell* us about it. The rigor with which Flaubert implemented this distinction constitutes a watershed in the history of narrative. *Madame Bovary* is the first novel to be narrated by the *authorial* voice of the writer composing the novel from fragments of human experience—from language—rather than by a narrator whose relationship to these experiences is analogous to our own.

The impersonality of *Madame Bovary* was not achieved merely by suppressing authorial interventions; there are in fact numerous editorial comments throughout the novel. Flaubert's narrative technique makes innovative use of a number of stylistic devices, the most notable of which are "free indirect discourse" and "typical narration."

Free Indirect Discourse

One of the most striking features of Flaubert's style is the new significance he gives to the ancient but previously aesthetically unmarked device of free indirect discourse. This technique is easier to illustrate than to explain, although its grammatical forms can be rigorously defined.

Direct discourse is quotation: "Mary was puzzled. She said [to herself], 'John loves me. How could he betray me?'"

Indirect discourse replaces the quotation with a subordinate clause: "Mary was puzzled. She said [to herself] that John loved her. She wondered how he could have betrayed her."

This example demonstrates the awkwardness of indirect discourse for the presentation of anything but actual speech. If Mary only thought these things but did not say them, there is no effective indirect form: "Mary thought that John loved her" does not say the same thing as "Mary thought, 'John loves me.'"

But Mary's situation is easily presented in free indirect discourse: "Mary was puzzled. John loved her. How could he have betrayed her?"

Here the author is not affirming that John loves Mary, merely that this is what Mary thinks. On the contrary, the text implies that Mary's assessment of the situation is illusory: John does not love her at all; his betrayal would be understandable to anyone but her. Yet this impression is conveyed to the reader by a series of simple sentences with no visible trace of irony. The outward simplicity of the free indirect form in comparison to either of the others masks a strange complexity in the status of its affirmations. The very stating of the character's thought as an objective fact implies that it is contrary to fact.

In this example, I have stacked the deck by including information that throws doubt on Mary's presuppositions. In an example like: "Mary caught the waiter's eye. She wanted a pastrami sandwich," we would interpret the sentence as a variant of ordinary indirect discourse—as the equivalent of "Mary said to the waiter, 'I want . . .'"

This was the traditional function of free indirect discourse before Flaubert. Flaubert often uses free indirect discourse in this way, even more frequently in his later novels than in *Madame Bovary*. But his stylistic originality comes from his exploitation of the problematic case where presenting the character's thoughts as the author's own implies their falsity rather than their truth.

Here is an example from the novel. The narrator is describing Emma's state of mind on her return home after her first experience of adultery—an experience about which the author wrote of his identification not only with Emma and Rodolphe, but with the horses and the trees:

> [Emma] repeated to herself: "I have a lover! a lover," exulting in this idea as though it were that of a new puberty that had come to her. *Thus she was finally going to possess those joys of love, that fever of happiness of which she had despaired. She was entering something marvelous where all would be passion, ecstasy, delirium; a bluish immensity surrounded her,* the summits of emotion shone beneath her thought, ordinary existence appeared only in the distance, far below, in the shadow, between the intervals of these heights. (part 2, chapter 9; my italics)

The first sentence uses direct discourse to describe Emma's thoughts, which are not illusory: she does indeed have a lover. The second illustrates Flaubert's use of free indirect discourse. The third makes a transition to an objective description of her imaginings: the words "beneath her thought" and "appeared" are correlates of ordinary rather than free indirect discourse. The following paragraph will make clear that the source of these desires is not Emma's unique personal history, but her readings of romantic novels.

We sense as we read this passage that Emma is not really "entering something marvelous." But how do we know this? Let us recall our previous example. We may take "Mary wanted a pastrami sandwich" to mean simply that she said, "I want a pastrami sandwich." Such a statement establishes its own truth. If Mary said this to the waiter, then whatever her inner feelings toward pastrami, she can objectively be said to want the sandwich. The credibility of the expression of desire is equivalent to the credibility of the sentence as pronounced by the character in context. The same is true for Emma's thoughts in the quoted passage. Emma cannot know that she is about to possess the fever of happiness, so we read the passage ironically. Yet the truth of the indirect quotation is never denied by the author. We may just as easily conclude that Emma was indeed about to possess the "fever of happiness," but this "fever" would be shown to be an illusion. The statement is "true," but its components are not what they seem to be; the language of desire is our only means of describing experience, but it inevitably falsifies this experience.

Free indirect discourse is not a mere grammatical mode, but a *rhetorical* form that makes us question the status of the author's statements concerning his character's subjective states. Here we find the underlying unity between literary technique and theme. As this passage well illustrates, Emma's desires have no original, personal content; they merely reproduce literary images. "*Those* joys of love, *that* fever of happiness" are not known to Emma through her own experience, but through the books she has read. Emma is not really open to empirical reality; she can only assimilate what she experiences to categories established in her mind by her knowledge of cultural fictions. Hence the status of a statement like "She was entering something marvelous" is essentially undetermined. We have no objective means of evaluating Emma's states of being. The use of free indirect discourse limits the narrator to the character's own categories of thought, categories that, in Emma's case, correspond to no possible experience of the reader, male or female. The Other as protagonist is not a potential partner in dialogue whom we might interrogate as to her feelings, or warn not to succumb to them. The irony of the quoted passage is not that Emma only *thought* she was about to possess the objects of her desire, but that these objects themselves are unreal.

Emma's desire frightens us by the sheer lack of lived substance that makes "something marvelous" a state we can imagine only in literary characters. The traditional narrator played the role of an intermediary between the character's mental categories and our own.

Flaubert's authorial use of free indirect discourse forces the reader to deal with the character in terms not of a common experience of life, but of a stock of romantic clichés that we, like Emma, know only through our reading of previous fictions.

"TYPICAL NARRATION"

Traditional narratives consist chiefly of scenes in which specific events are described from the standpoint of a more or less omniscient observer. The typical activities of the characters are recounted only in order to set the stage for these events. Although Flaubert by no means does away with the narration of events, he is the first novelist to treat typical scenes on the same level of importance with them. In so doing, he makes extended use of the imperfect tense which is used in French to recount such scenes.

The French imperfect tense is usually translated in English by the past progressive ("John was eating dinner when Mary entered the room") or by an expression of habitual past action ("John used to eat dinner at six o'clock"; "John would eat dinner at six o'clock"). The extended use of the imperfect in narrative is traditionally confined to passages that provide background for scenes of action narrated in the simple past or "preterit" tense ("John ate dinner and went out").

The distinction between imperfect and preterit corresponds roughly to that between previous knowledge and actual experience; the former is summed up, the latter narrated in detail as if we were reliving it for ourselves. This correspondence with the categories of ordinary experience reinforces our tendency to attribute traditional narration to a narrator-witness who, however much his knowledge of the character's lives and thoughts may exceed our own, experiences their world in the same time frame as the reader. Just as in everyday life, background is separated from foreground; what urgently attracts our attention is set off from what we know already. Flaubert's use of typical scenes narrated in the imperfect tense breaks down this apparently natural opposition. The voice that speaks in these scenes is not that of a narrator witnessing events or summing up past knowledge, but of an author revealing the essence of his characters' experiences from a standpoint unavailable within their own temporal perspective.

Let us examine a few examples of this technique from the early part of *Madame Bovary*. Although the imperfect in such passages is often translated by the English simple past, I have translated it here in such a way as to emphasize the specific meaning of the tense. These three passages, all written entirely in the imperfect, illustrate three degrees of radicality in the use of "typical narration."

1. Charles visits the house of Emma's father whose broken leg is healing (part 1, chapter 2):

> [Emma] would always accompany [Charles] to the bottom of the stoop. While his horse had not yet been brought, she would remain there. They had said good-bye, they were no longer speaking; the fresh air would surround her, lifting up pell-mell the little wild hairs on the nape of her neck, or making flutter on her hip the strings of her apron, which would twist like streamers. One time, when the snow was melting. . . .

This passage retains something of the time frame of conventional narrative. The repeated nature of the scene is stressed by the word "always," and the typical scene is followed by the narration of a specific incident beginning with the words "one time." There is nevertheless a concreteness about the typical scene that would have been unthinkable for Flaubert's predecessors. Could the wind have blown Emma's hair and apron strings every time? The scene is recounted not as a single event, but as the composite of an indefinite number of events. The absence of a witnessing narrator tempts us to refer the language of the narration to the unexpressed mental processes of the characters. Although the author is not reproducing the characters' thoughts as in the case of free indirect discourse, he may be said to be reproducing the kind of composite memory they would retain of an action repeated over time in slightly varying forms. This example is not a particularly radical use of typical narration, since the text suggests that Charles himself was aware that the mental scene in question consisted of a combination of several experiences. The repeated scene, described from his point of view, is memorable for him, and so we have some justification in imagining his remembrance of it.

2. Emma takes long walks with her dog, meditating on the inadequacy of her marriage (part 1, chapter 7):

> She would begin by looking all around, to see if anything had changed since the last time she had come. She would find in the same places the digitalis and the wallflowers, the clumps of nettles around the large stones. . . . Her thought, at first aimless, would wander at random, like her dog, who was describing circles in the countryside. . . . Then her ideas would gradually become focused and, sitting on the grass, which she would poke at with little strokes of the tip of her parasol, Emma would repeat to herself:
> —Why, my God, did I get married?

In this passage, repetition becomes a theme of the experience itself. Emma looks around each time to see if anything has changed. The very purpose of her walks is to solve the problem of marital boredom; repetition confirms this boredom rather than providing, as in the preceding passage, a reassuring demonstration of the meaningfulness of existence. Emma's awareness of repetition only aggravates her frustrated desire that something indeed be different. The sole appearance of a past tense other than the imperfect is in Emma's exclamation "Why, my God, did I get married?" Thus the only true event referred to in this passage is blamed for the uneventfulness that has followed.

It is even less possible here than in the first passage to imagine that on a number of separate occasions Emma had exactly the same thought while performing exactly the same action of poking the ground with her parasol. Nor is it useful to speak of the scene as a "composite memory." Charles (and perhaps Emma as well) may have reminisced about the tender adieux of the first passage, but the second scene is essentially self-contained. Emma need not *remember* these walks to feel their impact; their repeated uneventfulness is enough. The author is describing a kind of mental image for which we have no name; he crystallizes the essence of Emma's experience *for her*, but in terms neither she nor any human observer would have been able to employ.

3. Emma finds married life unbearable (part 1, chapter 9):

> But it was above all at mealtimes that she could no longer bear it, in that little room on the ground floor, with the smoking stove, the squeaking door, the damp tiles; all the bitterness of existence seemed to her to be served up on her plate, and, in the steam of the stew, there would rise from the depths of her soul something like other fumes of insipidity. Charles would take long to eat; she would nibble on a few hazelnuts, or else, leaning on her elbow, would amuse herself by tracing lines in the oilcloth with the point of her knife.

The third passage neither sets the stage for a specific event like the first nor attributes its typical nature to a willful act like the second. Emma chooses to take walks with her dog, but the repetition of dinner is beyond her control. This use of the technique of typical narration is, so to speak, tautological; the very fact of describing Emma's experience of such a necessarily repeated activity reveals a stifling uneventfulness. Is Emma specifically aware of the repetition of these scenes, or is each one sufficient in itself as an experience of frustration? Flaubert's technique makes this question unanswerable. Were this scene described as an *event*, or were it presented as a scene in a play, it would have to be taken as uniquely representative of other similar scenes. The technique of "typical narration" avoids this artificial transformation of the typical into the unique. Flaubert's detachment from the temporal structure of worldly action allows him to grant the uneventful the same degree of significance as the dramatic.

The claustrophobic effect of this passage would become the dominant mood of the naturalist novels of Émile Zola, who for this reason often strikes the modern reader as unfairly stacking the deck against his characters. A technique that was in Flaubert's hands the expression of a moment of particular frustration would be generalized as the expression of a worldview that inflexibly subordinated human aspirations to the limitations of material reality.

8

Flaubert's Realism

Flaubert admired neither the works nor the doctrines of the writers in his time who called themselves "realists." His reaction to critics' descriptions of his novel as "realist" was to claim that he had written *Madame Bovary* "out of hatred for realism."

It was nevertheless clear to the readers of his time that *Madame Bovary* carried out the realist program better than any of the productions of this marginal school. By the end of the nineteenth century, Flaubert's novels were spoken of by literary historians as the masterpieces of French realism, partly in order to differentiate them from the "naturalist" works of Zola and his disciples in the following generation. *Madame Bovary* is still described today as the exemplary realist novel.

A term as full of philosophical connotations as "realism" cannot be limited to a specific moment of literary history. The simplest definition of realism is as the attitude that sees things for what they are, in contrast with the romantic view that colors them with the illusions of what it would like them to be. *Madame Bovary* satisfies this commonsensical definition by debunking the illusions of romantic desire. Whether or not it makes sense to claim that Emma and Charles are more "real" than the characters of romantic novelists like George

Sand, Flaubert's evident intention is to show that Emma's romantic dreams, unlike those of Sand's protagonists, are not even conceivably realizable within the world of lived experience.

This permits us to define the literary realism of *Madame Bovary* in a less futile manner than by searching for the criteria of reality in the fictional text. Flaubert's realism consists in the existence of a contrast in kind between the character's desire and its worldly object. In a romantic work, the protagonist may, and usually does, fail to attain the object of his desires, but the authenticity of these desires is never put into question. If the real fails to correspond to the ideal, the fault is neither with the ideal nor with the real in a general sense, but with the state of reality at this particular moment. In naturalist works, the contrast between desire and reality is abolished from the opposite direction: instead of the world's being worthy of a noble desire, desire is degraded to a function of the "natural" world.

In Flaubert's universe, the world is not a very noble place, but the heroine's desires would be unrealistic in any possible world. Rodolphe and Léon are mediocre, but the lover Emma yearns for never existed anywhere but in romantic fiction. Realism in this sense portrays the world as real in opposition to a set of ideal expectations; the result is to devalue both halves of the opposition. Emma's ideal is not a justified yearning for something higher, but a romantic cliché. Yet at the same time, in contrast with that of *Don Quixote*, for example, Emma's world is criticized for its failure to live up to her expectations. In Flaubert's universe of infinite banality, where no dramatic conflict of significant forces takes place, Emma's longings provide the only possible form of transcendence, in a word the only possible *religion*.

It is clear from Flaubert's correspondence that one form of worldly activity escapes his condemnation: that of the artist. But art is not a part of the world, and is therefore not representable within it. In the world of *Madame Bovary*, Emma is as close as one gets to being an artist. Emma's ideals may be clichés, but her unhappy attempt to apply these ideals to her surroundings is the only possible form of worldly creativity.

Because Flaubert's novels contain many closely observed details of the life of his time, it was common until recently to emphasize the social (really, the sociological) aspect of his work. Today the pendulum has swung in the other direction; Flaubert is seen as a precursor of modern writers whose work purports to unmask the "realist illusion" of attributing reality to a fictional world.

Once we separate Flaubert's observation of the details of everyday life from the overall question of his role as a social observer, the contrast with true social novelists like Balzac or Dickens becomes obvious. Flaubert has no respect for the operations of the real world. In contrast to Balzac, who delighted in describing financial transactions, Flaubert only deals with the realities of the marketplace when it is absolutely necessary for his story. Both his correspondence and the text of the novel display his distaste for narrating any series of purposeful acts. For Flaubert, worldly success, rather than being the sign of superior force or even of superior ruthlessness, is the sign of a superior degree of *bêtise*. To succeed in the world is to be unable to stand above it, and the example of Homais shows that the most successful are the most monstrously conformist. The result of this attitude, much in evidence in *Madame Bovary* and still more dominant in Flaubert's later writings, is to drain of meaning all acts of goal-directed social or economic activity, reducing them to their immediate, often ridiculous appearances. It is because of this reductiveness that the Marxist critic Lukacs considered Flaubert a "decadent" writer in spite of his contempt for bourgeois society.

Flaubert's devaluation of worldly goals "de-realizes" the world of action by eliminating its only source of meaning. From this standpoint, Flaubert's very realism becomes a source of unreality, just as contemporary "hyperrealist" paintings that are drawn as accurately as photographs strike the observer as resembling not the scene they portray but a photograph of it. The more closely the details are observed, the less the whole picture of human intention is visible. Thus a modern novelist like Nathalie Sarraute, who narrates action in her novels as a series of tiny movements or "tropisms," can justifiably claim Flaubert among her literary ancestors.

Flaubert often spoke of his work as a form of "copying" reality. His posthumous last novel *Bouvard and Pécuchet* describes the misadventures of two retired copyists (clerical workers in an era before typewriters and Xerox machines) who, after an endless series of botched attempts at practical action, decide at last to return to copying. Only Flaubert's notes remain to tell us how the novel would have ended, but it appears that the pair would have begun by copying at random, and would later have turned to the compilation of lists of stupidities, the most famous of these being Flaubert's long-term project *Le Dictionnaire des idées reçues* [Dictionary of "received" ideas], which he apparently intended to integrate into the novel. For Flaubert, copying is not a passive activity; its very lack of intelligence subversively infects the objects it reproduces.

Flaubert is undoubtedly a precursor of the experimental novel of our century, but it would be a poor tribute to him to reduce him to this role. For if Flaubert's "copying" deprives its object of meaning less radically than that of such novelists as Sarraute or Alain Robbe-Grillet, this is because of what has been referred to as his "realist" aim of opposing the protagonist's desires to the world in which they must operate. The hopelessness of Emma's dreams for a uniquely meaningful life can only be demonstrated in a world governed by a recognizable set of common meanings. Even the most radical narrative, if it is not to break down into utter nonsense, must sustain an imaginary reality in the short term. Experimental novelists disconcert us by making it difficult or impossible to combine these short-term imaginations into a coherent whole. Flaubert's universe too may be called absurd, but one must be careful to distinguish between the absurdity of the banal and stupid and the more modern variety which makes everyday actions appear strange and disconcerting. Flaubert's study of the Otherness of desire can only be understandable in a world that retains the familiar feel of ordinary human experience.

9

Flaubert and
the Marketplace

The nineteenth century was the first period in history to be dominated
by the social structure of the *market*. The market is usually described
as a mechanism for exchanging goods; but the most fundamental market item is human labor. In a bourgeois world, individuals acquire
value from selling their services; each seeks to make himself as indispensable as possible. The majority of the population devote themselves to careers of producing and selling commodities, and it is they
who chiefly interest economists. But students of cultural activities are
concerned with the way in which the social predominance of the mar-
ket-mechanism affects human relations in general. Perhaps the most
fundamental explanation of the significance of *Madame Bovary* is that
it provides a new model for the understanding of human behavior in
market society.

Flaubert's world was not yet dominated like our own by communications media, advertising, and the related phenomena of consumer society. His work may nevertheless be said to anticipate these
developments. As with all great artists, artistic creation was for Flaubert a means of discovering models of behavior which were not yet
accessible to the theoretical consciousness of his time.

Flaubert's literary career would be inexplicable without the events of 1848–51. The failed revolution of 1848, which after three years of indecisive republicanism led to the establishment of the Second Empire under the harsh rule of Louis-Napoleon Bonaparte, was the watershed between the two halves of the century and between two major phases in the evolution of bourgeois society, not only in France but throughout Europe. The romantic movement of the first half of the nineteenth century vehemently opposed the inhumanity and "alienation" of the newly dominant market-system. But the characteristic romantic themes, the promotion of the unique experience of the Self and nostalgia for "natural" precapitalist forms of social organization, served in fact to provide the romantics and their readers with the psychological means of coming to terms with life in a market society.

In order to operate effectively within the market economy, where value is conferred by exchange rather than by established tradition or authority, the Self must possess a guarantee of its unique individuality independent of the market itself. The prolonged adolescence characteristic of the nineteenth-century bourgeoisie, later gradually extended to the working class, is a period of adaptation during which the young person not only acquires skills he will use in later life, but above all develops the modern sense of Self lacking in all earlier forms of social organization. The individual can no longer derive his understanding of the world and of his place in it from tradition and religious ritual; he must find it in his own intimate experience. The various styles of romantic nostalgia and exoticism, inevitably directed toward prebourgeois social forms, provide the Self with roots in a universe of values not determined by the market. It would be a naive error to confuse the romantics' predilection for tradition with tradition itself. In preindustrial times, tradition is invisible because it is universally accepted as the only way of doing things. The romantic does not lead a traditional life; he chooses to identify himself with primitive or aristocratic figures because they provide him with a sense of personal value, make him stand out in a universe of anonymous exchange.

Romanticism was an aesthetic mode, but it had distinct political implications. In the romantic utopia, each individual is a unique, valuable entity. No essential conflict exists in such a society, because the market ideally provides a means for realizing the unique potential of each of its participants.

Madame Bovary is the first fictional expression of a postromantic worldview. The author's political pessimism is obvious, but this is only the most superficial sign of the new vision this work expresses.

Only the Other's desire is real for Flaubert because he has lost all confidence in the desires of the romantic Self. The romantics thought that individual desire was the only guide to understanding the world. This faith is always expressed in opposition to the cold objectivity of the values of the market, but in fact it constitutes an uncritical promotion of them. Human desire is not an absolute given with its source in the individual; it is conditioned by the values that others attach to its objects. Its operation in market society is thus controlled by the marketplace where the collectivity determines the value of these objects. However much one believes the contrary, expressing confidence in desire is equivalent to expressing confidence in the market mechanism. By forcing himself to understand desire from without, Flaubert was attempting to separate himself from any direct contact with the market society that surrounded him.

The result is an analysis that Flaubert's contemporaries, the "realists" included, tended to see as unpardonably cold-blooded. Instead of being carried along in the romantic vision of the infinite productivity of desire, Flaubert was the first writer to become aware of its poverty. Emma's world is already a consumer society where the marketplace has captured the language and the attitudes of romantic desire for its own purposes. Although Emma yearns for love more than wealth, it is her failure to resist the blandishments of the sinister merchant Lheureux that precipitates the crisis that drives her to suicide.

The more naive romantics thought that by relying on their own intimate values they could resist the modern world's only real source of social value, the marketplace. Firm in this belief, they committed the strategic blunder of underestimating their adversary. The real greatness of romanticism lies not in its contempt for the market, but in its intuition that the structures of desire can serve the individual as a model for the organization of society as a whole. This intuition is best suited to lyric poetry, where the individual's uniqueness is not expressed in the worldly, temporal desire that is the novel's domain, but in the preworldly experience of intimacy. "Privacy" is in fact very much the creation of the bourgeois era. The creation of a protected personal universe is industrial society's way of preparing its young people to face the rigors of the market economy; but the extended adolescence that strengthens the ego gives the Self the sense of *place* that is fundamental to all human values, those of the market included. The greatest achievements of romanticism are the images of the Self's constitutive experiences, the figures of lost paradise that one finds in the great poets of the period.

Flaubert was the first novelist to recognize the limits of the romantic vision of desire. Romanticism's naive self-confidence prepared youth all too well for the bourgeois world, against which it left them no real defense. By exploring the romantic worldview in the context of the Other, Flaubert protected himself against its illusions in order better to expose them. But he does more than expose illusion; he shows that it is necessary for the functioning of the social order. Emma's pathological financial dealings with Lheureux are prophetic. They anticipate the twentieth-century search for buyable distinction, as typified by the consumption pattern of the contemporary "yuppie." Thorstein Veblen's analysis of this kind of behavior as "conspicuous consumption" in his *Theory of the Leisure Class* (1899) was further from the essence of the phenomenon than Flaubert had been forty years earlier. Such is the prophetic power of literary intuition.

Every aspect of *Madame Bovary*, from its choice of a female protagonist to its impersonal authorial style dominated by the technique of free indirect discourse, may be understood as an element of Flaubert's response to the new stage in market society that followed the catastrophic end of the romantic era in the events of 1848-51. This does not mean that the novel is a mere *product* of socioeconomic forces. It explores consequences of these forces which no economic or political theoretician could have detected at the time.

Flaubert and the Marketplace

Flaubert's critique of market society, far more radical than that of the romantics, is nonetheless ultimately in complicity with it; no human creation can be altogether independent of the social system in which it is created. But this complicity is no longer, as that of the romantics may be said to have been, a preparation for success in the market. Léon, the prototypical young romantic bourgeois, leaves the insolvent Emma and marries an heiress in his quest for prosperity. But in Flaubert's world such achievements are not merely condemned, they are made to appear altogether uninteresting. If the romantics may be said to have prepared their readers for worldly triumph, Flaubert's work provides them with a consolation for worldly failure. Like the pessimistic philosophy of Arthur Schopenhauer that became popular in France in his later years, Flaubert presents the practical world as itself a place of illusion. The unending failures of the twin heroes of *Bouvard and Pécuchet* lead them toward the only form of worldly success Flaubert could conceive of in nineteenth-century bourgeois society: copying, mocking yet fascinated imitation, a model of "realist" art.

In Flaubert's vision of the world, the artist occupies a privileged position. But unlike the romantic, the postromantic artist can serve only marginally as a model of worldly behavior; he succeeds in art only by his invisibility in the world. This vision retains its attractiveness for us today because we remain aware of what Flaubert already glimpsed about advanced market societies: their generation in their members of a constant anxiety of success. In a competition over signs of distinction rather than material needs, few can confidently claim to have succeeded, but many know well that they have failed. Flaubert's novels, beginning with *Madame Bovary,* are studies not in tragic defeat but in failure. The market-society generates desires that are apparently fulfillable, because they are directed at articles of consumption; but the real objects of these desires lie always beyond our reach. Emma is not incapable of action; she purchases luxury goods and has real love affairs. But neither the affairs nor the goods can satisfy her. Emma's failure dramatizes that of all the Selves-as-Others, the satisfied/unsatisfied members of modern consumer society.

10

The Aftermath of
Madame Bovary

THE TRIAL

Madame Bovary was the object of one of the two most celebrated literary trials of nineteenth-century France, both of which took place in 1857. Flaubert was acquitted; Charles Baudelaire was less fortunate. Although it is easy to understand how the explicit sexuality of some of Baudelaire's poems might have shocked a conservative jury, the reasons for which Flaubert's novel, which strikes us today as anything but pornographic, was accused of offending "public and religious morality" are not absolutely clear.

With the encouragement of his friend Maxime du Camp, Flaubert published *Madame Bovary* in installments in the *Revue de Paris,* beginning in October 1856. This liberal literary journal, of which Du Camp was an editor, was not in the good graces of Napoleon III's regime. Many, beginning with Flaubert himself, have interpreted the prosecution as little more than an attempt to harass the journal and to force it to shut down (something that was in fact accomplished only a few months later). Most scholars now conclude, however, that there is no need to attribute the prosecution to ulterior motives; Flaubert's novel was indeed scandalous to the more traditional sectors of society.

In any case, *Madame Bovary* could not have furnished a credible pretext for indictment had it not offended the moral sensibilities of an important fraction of the population.

The trial was held on 31 January and 7 February 1857. Flaubert's lawyer, Jules Senard (the correct spelling according to Jean Bruneau), to whom he later dedicated the novel, was a prestigious figure, a former president of the National Assembly during the short-lived Second Republic. Louis-Napoleon's regime was, in contemporary terms, authoritarian but not totalitarian. Despite the fact that the government itself had brought the accusation, Flaubert and his codefendants, the *Revue's* director Léon Laurent-Pichat and its printer Auguste-Alexis Pillet, were acquitted with only a verbal rap on the knuckles by the judge. Although Flaubert experienced the trial as a humiliation, the attendant publicity contributed considerably to spreading the fame of the novel. When *Madame Bovary* appeared in book form in April 1857, it sold 15,000 copies in two months.

What then was so scandalous about *Madame Bovary*? The prosecuting attorney, whose summation is less than half as long as that of the defense and considerably less rhetorical, pointed to certain passages in the novel, like Emma's exclaiming "I have a lover!" after her seduction by Rodolphe, as examples of an overly positive view of adultery. The death scene came in for condemnation because of its liturgically correct but nevertheless undoubtedly suggestive allusions to Emma's illicit loves.

But there was something in this novel far more disturbing to public morality than a few suggestive passages: its impersonal "authorial" narration that presented a fictional universe without a filter of implicit or explicit moral values. Both sides, for lack of a better term, referred to this as the novel's "realism." Ernest Pinard, the prosecutor, was perspicacious enough to note that although Emma is surely punished for her sins, she has no moral superior in the novel. As he put it, "There is not in the book one character who can condemn her . . . who can make her bow her head." The other characters are either too weak, like Charles, or too ridiculous, like Homais or the priest Bournisien. The defense never really answered this objection, preferring to evoke the suffering visited on Emma as a result of her crimes as a sufficient guarantee of the novel's moral tenor.

The most revealing point in the trial arguments is the analysis of the cause of Emma's predicament, an analysis on which both sides agree. Her fundamental flaw is that she has received an education "above her station" and is thus unable to accept, as she should, her mediocre lot in life. The prosecution and the defense both anticipate Jules de Gaultier's definition of "Bovarysm" as the desire to be other than one is, without sharing Gaultier's appreciation for Bovarysm's positive side. Seen in the perspective of Flaubert's time, this is a reasonable interpretation: Emma aspires too high, lets her youthful readings and her dance with the Viscount go to her head. But we would hardly continue to read the novel today if it were a mere period piece about the condition of a provincial woman in the nineteenth century. Emma aspires above her station because the culture in which she lives no longer prepares its members to remain in "their station."

Flaubert saw far more acutely than either his defender or his accuser the incipient consumerism of his world. Emma may be "over-educated" for a farm girl, but she is anything but an awkward bumpkin trying to fit into sophisticated society. When Rodolphe first sees her, he finds her "turned out like a Parisienne." This does not mean we should adopt the contrary position and claim that Emma is indeed too good for her mediocre surroundings, like the peasant's beautiful daughter who marries the prince in the fairy tale. Emma is indeed a farm girl, but she already lives in a world where a farm girl can read magazines and become as chic as anyone else. Emma's problems, in short, are not those of a rigidly stratified community where one is born and dies in one's "station," but those of a world moving in the direction of the relatively classless societies of our own century, where satisfaction with one's current lot is the exception rather than the rule.

The prosecution recognized that Emma was punished for her inappropriate aspirations, but complained that these aspirations themselves were nowhere explicitly condemned; Emma fails, but never has to "bow her head." The defense could only answer lamely that in view of Emma's unhappy end, the young woman who reads this novel will presumably hesitate before following her example. But Flaubert had understood that the entire industrialized world was in the process of following Emma's example. Not only would the modern economy collapse without Bovarysm, but it is unclear, to say the least, what objective basis is available for condemning those who "see themselves as other than they are." No society more than ours justifies Gaultier's exaltation of Bovarysm as the source of human progress.

FLAUBERT AFTER *MADAME BOVARY*

Although *Madame Bovary* would remain the best known and most widely read of his writings, Flaubert continued to produce major works of fiction until his death in 1880. Always an agonizingly slow and painstaking writer, Flaubert finished only two other full-length novels in his lifetime. His second, *Salammbô* (1862), a gory, carefully researched historical novel about ancient Carthage, is more a curiosity than a masterpiece. But his following book, the second *Sentimental Education* (1869), is one of the summits of nineteenth-century fiction. A more nuanced and complex work than *Madame Bovary,* it tells the story of a young man whose romantic dreams of bliss make him incapable of action. The novel is set in Paris before, during, and after the revolutionary events of 1848; with satiric relish, Flaubert draws parallels between the self-indulgent fiasco of the hero's life and the recent history of the French nation as a whole. *Sentimental Education* was the author's own favorite among his works, and he was deeply disappointed at its relative lack of popularity after the succès de scandale of his first novel.

Flaubert was shaken by France's humiliating defeat at the hands of the Prussians in 1870 and appalled at the popular uprising of the Paris Commune that followed. But the humiliation of the French bourgeoisie that had begun with the coup d'état twenty years earlier came to an end in 1871 with the inauguration of the Third Republic, which would endure until another German invasion in 1940. With the disappearance of the social order that had provided a justification for his withdrawal from worldly action, Flaubert's literary perspective changed. Henceforth his protagonists would be worldly analogues of the artist, but he would never complete another novel.

In 1872 Flaubert produced a final, much shorter version of *The Temptation of Saint Anthony*, which offers a pantheistic identification with material reality in all its forms as a solution to the temptations of worldly desire. *Three Tales*, which appeared in 1877, was Flaubert's last publication during his lifetime. Set in the three epochs of Christian history, the biblical (*Herodias*), the medieval (*Saint Julian the Hospitaler*), and the modern (*A Simple Heart*), these stories are meditations on the possibilities of intraworldly salvation in which the saint's role can be read as an allegory of that of the writer.

Flaubert's last years were darkened by financial distress brought on in 1875 by the business failure of the husband of his beloved niece. Toward the end, this proud, independent figure was obliged to accept a government sinecure in order to keep his residence in Croisset. Although beset by a growing sense of isolation, Flaubert in the 1870s came increasingly to be looked up to as a model by the next generation of French novelists.

When Flaubert died suddenly of a stroke in 1880 at the age of fifty-eight, he had nearly completed the satiric novel *Bouvard and Pécuchet* on which he had been working since 1873. But this is no ordinary novel. The series of misadventures experienced by the two "copyist" heroes in their encyclopedic quest for knowledge and expertise permits the author to deride the futility of all worldly endeavors and the silliness of their various jargons. After experiencing failure and disillusionment at every turn, the pair was to return to their original profession of copying, beginning first at random but gradually transforming their work into the compilation of lists of published stupidities, of which their creator had himself compiled a goodly number. But the exact form of the novel Flaubert would have published had he lived to complete it remains a mystery; nor is it certain that he would, or could, ever have completed it. For by returning to their copying-desk, the twin heroes would have become virtually indistinguishable from the novelist himself, who by definition could never write "The End" to his own story. *Bouvard and Pécuchet* is best thought of as an *essentially* unfinished work.

CONCLUSION: THE LESSON OF FLAUBERT

Flaubert neither loved nor admired mankind as a whole. Ingenious critics like Sartre and Jonathan Culler have interpreted his entire literary career as an endeavor to avenge himself on humanity by demoralizing his readers. But if we recall Flaubert's own dictum that stupidity consists in making judgmental conclusions about reality, we are likely to arrive at a more balanced view. Every great creator is both a discoverer and an inventor of human truth, and such truths necessarily cut both ways.

On the negative side, Flaubert shows that the modern world is no longer a traditional community even to the limited extent in which the fraternal bond between narrator and reader had preserved this community on the cultural plane. Henceforth all readings will be subjective: one will never be sure to what extent they are shared by others, to what extent any writing is really "readable," even by the author himself. This perspective extends to human relations in general. In the contemporary world, value systems are increasingly subjectivized; each individual is entitled to his or her own set of religious and moral beliefs, with only the mass media providing a degree of social cohesion. But the media, whose truth-irrelevant language Flaubert anticipated, accomplish this task not by imposing a uniform standard on everyone, but by offering a menu of values from which each may choose the ones he likes. In such a world, it no longer seems possible to distinguish between the authentic and inauthentic use of language, or even between authentic and inauthentic human relationships.

But it is possible to take a more positive outlook on the modern world. The consumer society Flaubert anticipated in *Madame Bovary* is founded on the continued proliferation of highly differentiated goods and services out of which each consumer is encouraged to create a unique "consumption profile" of his or her own. This ostensibly materialistic social order offers its members a chance to become, on the very basis of the cultural discourses of advertising and the media, unique individuals different not only from everyone else, but from any fixed image they may have of themselves. Each person's insistence on his or her unique individuality makes personal relationships more problematic, but potentially more rewarding, just as our awareness of the difficulty of reading texts has made our critical discourse more sensitive to the human truths they contain.

Madame Bovary demonstrates in its own terms that Freud's famous question "What does a woman want?" can only be answered intelligently if we take it to mean "What does the Other want?" The world of *Madame Bovary* is one in which all Selves are Others, understandable only from without, from an "authorial" rather than a "narrative" perspective. For Flaubert, writing in nineteenth-century France, a woman's desires are something with which he cannot immediately identify on the basis of his own experience, but which can only be understood as the product of a set of cultural discourses. But his novel expresses the more universal intuition that all the participants in the modern world he anticipated have become so differentiated from one another that no one's subjectivity can be immediately available to anyone else.

Sexual difference is only the most obvious example of the human difference that modern market society cultivates and without which it could not survive. The final lesson of *Madame Bovary* is that all human understanding is based on our acceptance of one another's Otherness. Emma fails because she takes the cultural discourses of her time at their word as fixed models of experience, as though they provided an answer to questions like Freud's. Our post-Flaubertian and post-Freudian society will only remain viable so long as it continues to afford us the means of never having to answer such questions, of never having to presume to know in advance what any Other is capable of desiring, including ourselves.

Analysis of
Selected Passages

11

Part 1

OPENING SEQUENCE (CHAPTER 1)

We were in study hall, when the Headmaster entered, followed by a new boy dressed in street clothes (*habillé en bourgeois*) and a monitor carrying a large desk. Those who were sleeping awoke, and everyone stood up, as if surprised in his work.

The opening sequence of the novel, roughly the first three fifths of the first chapter, comes as a surprise to most new readers of *Madame Bovary*. After all one has heard about the new impersonality of Flaubert's narrative, one hardly expects him to begin his novel in the first person. The shadowy, collective "we" who disappears after these first pages seems to occupy a transitional position between the romantic self so apparent in Flaubert's earlier works and the impersonal narrator of the rest of the novel.

The novel opens with Charles's first appearance in the narrator's classroom. His entry is presented as a mock-dramatic event. Everyone stands up, but only because this is the custom whenever the headmaster enters the room. Charles is the new element in the situation, but the sentence that describes his entrance sandwiches him between the headmaster and the boy carrying the desk. This style of narration, typical of Flaubert, may be called *phenomenological*. Traditionally, introductions of narrative protagonists present some essential feature that sets them off from others. Flaubert's schoolboy-narrator is satisfied merely to describe the *phenomena* that he perceives in the order of their perception. The three persons who enter the room are presented in the order of their entry, which is also that of the school hierarchy. The headmaster comes to introduce Charles to the class, the monitor to carry his desk; neither will play any role in the narrative that follows. Yet Charles's central position in the group, rather than making him stand out, only hides him in the least significant position in the sentence, neither at the beginning nor at the end of the enumeration.

The expression *habillé en bourgeois,* literally "dressed as a bourgeois" but meaning simply that Charles is not wearing the school uniform, adds to the irony of the description. The word "bourgeois" was a term of derision for the artists and writers of Flaubert's generation. The bourgeoisie is precisely the middle class, standing between the two extremes here represented by the powerful headmaster and the monitor who is no more than a servant. Balzac had presented the middle-class protagonists of his novels in heroic, even Homeric terms. Flaubert even more than Balzac focuses his attention on this class; the protagonists of all his novels are bourgeois of one kind or another. But here as elsewhere, their importance is the paradoxical result of their mediocrity. The center is merely a middle. Charles is not the subject of the sentence; he appears in a subordinate clause as the derived subject of the verb "to follow." He is important precisely because he utterly fails to stand out.

The next few paragraphs present Charles at his moment of greatest difference from the other students. The narrator explains that the "in" thing to do was to throw one's cap on the floor on entering the classroom. Charles's ignorance of this procedure draws attention to his cap, which is described in one of Flaubert's most famous paragraphs:

> It was one of those composite pieces of headgear, where one finds
> features of the bearskin, the lancer cap, the derby hat, the otter-skin

cap and the nightcap, in short, one of those poor things whose mute
ugliness has depths of expression like an imbecile's face.

This passage is followed by a detailed description of the cap,
which has inspired a number of illustrators.

Charles's cap seems to belong more in a universe of satiric fantasy
than in a provincial schoolroom. The key word in the description is
"composite." The cap belongs to no single genre; it is military, sport-
ing, businesslike, and intimate all at once, a literary image whose very
incoherence makes it memorable. This mediocrity gone wild reveals a
failed aspiration at synthesis, as though Charles's cap had taken on
the mission of reconciling all the conflicts of the social order and had
failed in the most ridiculous fashion to accomplish its task.

The cap may thus be taken as a symbol of mediocrity, of failure;
but the very incoherence of this "symbol" implies the uselessness of
attempting a close interpretation of its meaning. It introduces us to a
world where the "middle" has taken into itself in an indifferent jumble
all the meaningful values that specific symbols had previously desig-
nated. Thus an attempt to reconstruct these meanings through a detailed analysis of the cap's construction would miss the author's point.
A similar effect has been obtained in our time by phenomena like pop
art, which by "quoting" earlier symbolic values do away with any
commitment to their meaning, reducing them to a flat set of arbitrary
styles.

Charles is set apart from the other boys in this classroom scene.
He accidentally drops his cap on the floor, then becomes the object of
further hilarity by his graceless pronunciation of his name as "Char-
bovari." But once the teacher has quieted the class by a punitive copying assignment, the scene ends quietly with his assurance to Charles
that he has not lost his cap. In the following paragraph, the narration
switches to an omniscient mode to describe Charles's family background and childhood. After the background narration has been
brought up to the time of Charles's arrival in the lycée, the personal
narrator of the opening scene makes his last appearance in the novel

in the following curious passage:

> It would be impossible now for any of us to recall anything about him. He was a boy of moderate temperament, who played during recreation, worked in study hall, listened in class, slept well in the dormitory and ate well in the dining room.

The contrast with Charles's central role in the opening scene could hardly be more explicit. At that point, Flaubert took pains to ensure that Charles would be distinguished from the other boys by more than the mere fact of being new at school; his unique cap is the sign of this concern. Charles was presented at first as exemplary in his mediocrity and the object of his classmates' mockery. He seemed cut out to be the class scapegoat. Yet once this scene is past, he becomes so inconspicuous that none of his classmates can remember anything about him.

The point of this passage is twofold. On the level of form, it justifies the transition from a personal to an impersonal narrator; if the first would be unable to remember anything about Charles, then only the second is able to narrate his story. But its thematic function is more important. Charles is not, after all, the main character in the novel; the title has already told us this. The inconspicuousness of his "central" position in the opening sentence demonstrates the paradox of exemplary mediocrity. In the category of the mediocre—which is for Flaubert characteristic of modern life in general—the most exemplary figure is not an individual set apart but someone altogether anonymous. The brief parody of the persecution of the romantic hero with which the novel begins is a flash in the pan; whether or not he continues to wear his cap, Charles will never again be singled out in any way by anyone. Flaubert is showing us that the complacent romantic image of the persecuted self, which goes back to Rousseau's *promeneur solitaire* (solitary walker), no longer offers a valid basis for a narrative. What appears to be exceptional is exceptional only in its averageness, and therefore not really exceptional at all.

The reader need not infer this abstractly. In the opening scene,

Charles is indeed picked on by the other boys, but his suffering never goes beyond laughter and a few spitballs. This scene therefore takes on the character not of a lynching but of an initiation. By entering the classroom, Charles becomes a member of civil society. His cap exemplifies the overblown quest for social unity that had characterized the bourgeoisie of the romantic period and that had been abandoned after 1851. To enter the world is to take off these illusions and throw them in the dirt as the other boys had learned to do.

We may now give a fuller interpretation of the role of Flaubert's unexpected personal narrator. Charles is observed at the outset by one of his potential persecutors, someone who never identifies himself as an individual but hides behind the mask of the student body as a whole. This collective "we" exists only in opposition to Charles in his pre-initiate state at the outset of the novel. It incarnates the social vision of an essentially powerless group bound together by certain norms (such as throwing one's cap against the wall), and slyly subversive of the rules imposed by its superiors (such as sleeping in study hall). Charles never really joins this group; in study hall, he studies, just as he dines in the dining hall and sleeps in the dormitory (in French, *dortoir*, from *dormir*, to sleep). He is never described as throwing his cap against the wall, but neither does he become the class scapegoat. For this schoolboy society has only a semblance of coherence. Unable to persecute those who fail to obey its norms, it merely forgets about them. These boys already resemble the conformist–nonconformist adolescents of our own era, all "different" in the same way. In this context, Charles's difference from the others grants him no mark of real distinction. Flaubert's world is one where distinction even in the broadest sense, specificity of any kind, is neither an inherent nor an acquired trait; it is something ever sought after but never attained.

The prolonged adolescence celebrated in romantic novels allowed young men to strengthen their sense of self in preparation for their entry into the marketplace. *Madame Bovary* belongs to an era in which the individual's primary role in the market is becoming that of consumer rather than producer; his preparation takes the form of a collective commitment to acquiring empty marks of distinction. Charles is not yet a part of this new world as Emma will be. He enters the scene as a mock-romantic hero, different from his fellows; but his real difference from them is his lack of awareness of the need to be different. The personal narrator of the early pages is needed in order to demonstrate the bankruptcy of the romantic mode of opposition between the unique central self and the peripheral mass. The transition to the impersonal narration of the body of the novel emphasizes the author's separation from the world he describes. Because the first narrator spoke with a voice that could be situated in the world, the voice of the second is shown by contrast to be detached from it.

The point is not that the author sees more in Charles than his contemporaries who have forgotten him. It is rather that Charles's lack of interest in being different makes him invisible to anyone but a narrator who has no stake in worldly differences. Charles is no one special; but Flaubert's narrator sees no one as special. The reader can understand and identify with Charles's modest desires in these early pages, but that is precisely why Charles cannot be the real protagonist of the novel. His indifference to distinction makes him incapable of incarnating the new consumption-driven model of desire. Emma is no more memorable than Charles, but she is motivated by a more radical desire for distinction than the pseudoromantic adolescents of the opening pages. Charles's simple desires are transparent to us; in Emma we will find a character whom we will not be able to understand from within, since all her ideas are acquired from without. Charles's desires will lead us to Emma, under whose attraction we will remain for the remainder of the novel.

First Visions of Emma (Chapter 2)

Charles has completed his medical studies and is married to a supposedly well-off widow some years his senior. One night he is called out to repair a farmer's broken leg and makes the acquaintance of Emma Rouault, the farmer's daughter. Emma is described through a series of minor incidents that reveal her character as if to a curious observer. The contrast with the opening presentation of Charles is instructive. Here the narrator is no longer identified with the "we" of the opening pages; Emma becomes the central object of the narration because she interests Charles, who is at this point the main character in the novel. It is remarkable that Flaubert will follow a similar procedure in Emma's first meetings with both Léon and Rodolphe; in each case, Emma is shown to us through the man's eyes.

This is Emma's first appearance in the novel (if we exclude the "letter sealed with blue wax" that she had sent to bring Charles to her father's bedside):

> A young woman, wearing a blue merino dress adorned with three flounces, came to the doorway of the house to receive M. Bovary, whom she invited into the kitchen, where a large fire was burning.

Charles first appeared in the novel as he entered the door of the classroom. Emma first appears to him as inviting him to enter. Charles was first seen as an intruder, an object of scorn; Emma welcomes him in from a chilly night to a warm fire. Whereas Charles's central position in the opening scene devalued his entrance by placing him between two other figures, Emma stands by herself at the goal of Charles's journey. And in contrast to Charles, whose awkward clothing had been topped with a ridiculous cap, Emma dresses elegantly, perhaps too elegantly for the occasion. The blue of her dress repeats that of her sealing wax; this color, which symbolizes naive idealism, serves throughout the novels as a leitmotiv of Emma's illusions of romantic fulfillment. The three flounces (in French, *volants,* with a suggestion of flying) might be seen by a symbolically minded reader as referring to the three loves that will dominate her existence; they suggest at the very least a certain capriciousness.

Emma's second appearance comes a few lines later, as Charles supervises the preparation of splints for M. Rouault's fracture:

> . . . Mlle Emma was attempting to sew pads [to put under the splints]. As she was a long time in finding her sewing kit, her father became impatient; she did not answer; but, as she sewed, she pricked her fingers, which she then put to her mouth to suck.
>
> Charles was surprised at the whiteness of her nails. They were shiny, narrow at the ends, rubbed cleaner than Dieppe ivories, and

cut in almond-shape. Yet her hand was not beautiful, not pale enough, perhaps, and a bit dry at the knuckles; it was too long as well, and without soft inflections in its contours. What was beautiful about her were her eyes: although they were brown, they appeared black because of the lashes, and her look came frankly at you with a candid boldness.

Here we get to know Emma a little more intimately. The first paragraph demonstrates her problematic relationship to her household duties. Her slowness in finding her sewing kit reveals less a lack of enthusiasm than a certain pretentiousness, as though she could not be expected to remember where so banal an article might be. In reaction to her father's complaints (note the use of free indirect discourse: M. Rouault must have *expressed* his impatience—the author is not merely describing his mental state), she neither answers in kind nor apologizes, but indulges in the masochistic act of pricking her fingers. Emma's first act in the novel is one that makes her both persecutor and victim, the drawer of her own blood. Charles temporarily became the victim of his fellows because of his difference from them; but he has no real desire to distinguish himself, and ultimately becomes an object of indifference. Emma's involuntary gesture shows her to be unconsciously attuned to life in a more modern world, where one becomes a victim only through one's own efforts. But whereas Charles, as a male, was the object of attention of a crowd, Emma can play this role only in an intimate setting, for a man's benefit.

The description of Emma in the first paragraph is focused in a manner not found in traditional narration, and which we have not seen in the descriptive passages devoted to Charles and his family. Balzac would have described his heroine from head to toe, and most likely interrupted the narration to inform us about her history and that of her parents. Had he wished to show us what Charles thought of her, he would have described not Emma's appearance but Charles's thoughts. Flaubert describes Emma only through details of her appearance that might have impressed Charles, but which are not explicitly attributed to him. This description includes an example of "typical narration": the imperfect tense that Flaubert uses here could be translated "she would prick her fingers." The author is not presenting his heroine to us either as a participant in an event or as a being defined by a set of stable traits of character. What we see can only be the result of external observation, focused on Emma for a certain length of time. When, in the following paragraph, Charles is specifically referred to as Emma's observer, we assume that her act of putting her fingers to her mouth attracted his notice unconsciously, so to speak. Charles's presence in the scene is less as an observing consciousness than as a point of identification for the reader, a temporary substitute for the absent "authorial" narrator.

This small-scale use of typical narration reveals what we might call the "consumerism" of Flaubert's narrative. There is no objective, collective set of values against which Emma's acts can be measured; they are only of interest within the immediate situation, in which they acquire a *value*, become an object of desire for someone within the world of the novel. The impersonal narrator denies all responsibility for the creation of such values; he speaks not in his own right but as though translating the thoughts of the characters into a language whose authenticity he steadfastly refuses to vouch for. We may find in Emma's pricking her fingers a symbolism undetected by Charles, the revelation of an unconscious sado-masochism driven by the need to see herself as a victim of her unprestigious surroundings. But our ability to interpret her acts is contingent on their possessing a local significance, or in economic terms, a "marginal utility" for Charles in the context in which he finds himself. Charles may not understand Emma's actions as we do, but he is attracted by them; they stimulate his desire, and he will remain fascinated by her throughout the novel.

Emma's mystery for Charles can be expressed in sexual terms (woman as the Other), but it is also useful to interpret the contrast between this passage and the introduction of Charles as revealing a *historical* difference between the two. Charles's aborted victimization and the peaceful anonymity that eventually follows show him to belong to a period when the Self presented itself immediately, naively, to the world. Emma already inhabits a society where selves are defined by the self-images they cultivate.

The second paragraph explicitly makes Charles the observer.

What strikes him is not Emma's masochistic act of pricking her fingers, but the whiteness of her nails, which has rather a sadistic connotation. Unable to fathom the complexity of her at once self-punishing and self-nourishing gesture, Charles is attracted to a sign of Emma's potential for cruelty, which at the same time illustrates another aspect of modern narcissism (as witness the proliferation of nail salons in our own time).

Yet taken as a whole, her hand is not beautiful. This observation seems more the author's than Charles's; but it can only be justified in context if we assume that Charles's attention, drawn at first to Emma's hand by her gesture, was then taken by her eyes. The hand is not sufficient to hold his interest. It is too dry, too long, not pale or well-rounded enough; in a word, a hand more masculine than feminine. Yet it is the activity of this hand that has drawn Charles's attention in the first place. He is struck by the care lavished on the nails, but the hand itself is incongruous because it appears as an active force rather than the feminine recipient of similar care. This points up the essential contradiction in Emma's role. In the Rouault farmhouse, there is no one for whom Emma is the central object of attention; she does not even have a maid. She is obliged to "make things happen," as her pricking her fingers suggests. Lacking the luxury of playing the passive, feminine role, Emma must play the active, male part as well. Her unrefined hand is the sign of this duality.

But the attractive force of Emma's eyes turns this ambiguity into an advantage. Their real color is brown, the least distinguished of eye colors, but they appear black because of the lashes, which must therefore be unusually long or thick. (At certain points in the novel, Flaubert will describe Emma's eyes as blue, or at least as appearing blue: her reality is one that adapts itself to masculine desire.) Emma gains a mysterious exotic quality from the fact that her eyes are partly hidden. Yet the most salient aspect of their charm is the boldness of their glance. The secret, feminine darkness of her eyes is coupled with a masculine candor of expression. The same ambivalence that makes her hand less than beautiful makes her eyes particularly attractive. By looking frankly at her interlocutor, she makes him aware that he is unable to see clearly the color of her eyes. By means of this open/secret look Emma expresses her interest in the Other; but what she displays is not her desire to see but the mystery of not quite being seen. Her observer has the exciting sensation of being invited to unveil a secret of which still more remains hidden.

This concentration on eye and hand is no accident. Eye–hand coordination is the basis for the practical intelligence by which our species dominates its environment. The hand performs, and the eye evaluates and corrects the performance. But as we have just seen, Emma is not particularly skillful with her hands. (In Flaubert's notes for the novel, he insists that Emma is not a gifted pianist, although he makes her a good dancer.) No doubt Emma pricks her fingers while sewing in order to punish/nourish herself, but a skilled seamstress would find another outlet for her frustrations. Emma seems betrayed rather than served by the relationship between eye and hand. She sees herself too much, is too self-conscious to become skilled in action. But in contrast, she becomes attractive to Charles because her eyes express to him her inner ambivalence. Flaubert insists on the *communicative* nature of this look that "came at *you* with a candid boldness." Emma's consciousness, which is not focused on her work, is free to be focused on others, in particular those who appear to offer her a possibility of escape from her surroundings.

The eye is the seat of desire, the hand the instrument of action. Emma is unskillful in action because her desire goes beyond the concrete objects that her practical abilities can master. Her hand is not beautiful because she cannot be fully either an active force or an aesthetic object; her eyes are attractive because their boldness forces the man who looks into them to play the active role of seeking for their true nature. But behind the eyelashes lies not mystery but the emptiness of romantic illusions that are as yet only indirectly suggested.

EMMA'S ADOLESCENCE (CHAPTER 6)

The chapter that describes Emma's youth is one of the most celebrated in the novel. In order to document the sources of his heroine's romantic attitudes, Flaubert plowed through piles of sentimental literature of the sort Emma might have read. Since Emma is a character with no immediate source in the author's experience, one who incarnates the Other, the description of her adolescent readings is of particular importance: Flaubert can define his heroine's desires only to the extent that these desires are determined by cultural practices.

This "cultural determinism" makes Emma's relation to life that of a consumer rather than a producer. Although she no longer lives in a traditional world where one's destiny is determined in advance, her literary models are taken from reconstructions of such a world. The science fiction and fantasy literature so popular with young readers today illustrates the same principle; whether or not it purports to take place in the future, its characters almost inevitably inhabit a universe as "medieval" as that of the novels Emma read as a girl.

The comparison has often been made between Emma and Don Quixote, who was also a great reader of romances and who like her attempted to construct his own life on the basis of his readings. But the Don actively transforms the reality he encounters (an ugly peasant girl) into the elements of his fictions (the beautiful Dulcinea). Emma's relation to reality remains always passive; rather than acting on the basis of her fantasies, she expects the men on whom she pins her hopes to act them out for her. Thus whereas Quixote can always interpret his experiences in accordance with his ideal, Emma goes from disappointment to disappointment.

Flaubert's choice of a female protagonist allows him to pinpoint the key feature of postromantic adolescence: its preparation of the young person to play a part less in a system of production than in a system of consumption. In the consumption-driven social order that was just coming into existence in Flaubert's time, the female role is in advance of the male. The modern Other-Self consumes objects in order to create an image of her/himself for the "consumption" of others. The self becomes more Other than Self, more a desirable object than a desiring subject. The contemporary male who wears colorful clothes and has his hair styled rather than cut pays homage to the woman's leading role in consumer society.

The introduction of Emma's background obeys on a larger scale the same pattern as that of Charles. We first met Charles through the eyes of an anonymous classmate; then we were introduced to his boy-hood, which chronologically preceded the opening scene. Similarly, we make Emma's acquaintance through Charles, and only later—after their marriage—learn of her experiences prior to their meeting. One thing Charles and Emma have in common, which is seldom remarked because the author never makes an explicit point of it, is that both are only children. This element of solitude allows Flaubert to emphasize the adolescent's distance from the rivalries of the adult world. His own adolescence, as his youthful literary works reveal, had been dominated by jealousy of his elder brother; in *Madame Bovary* he allows his char-acters to avoid all questions of competition within the family unit. The protagonists of Flaubert's fictional world tend not to compete with others, but to seek a domain where they can fancy themselves unique. This is another facet this universe has in common with modern con-sumer society, where each individual tries to define for himself a unique life-style that shields his delicate ego from the rough and tum-ble of direct competition with his fellows.

The sixth chapter is situated shortly after Emma's wedding, when she begins to realize that marriage to Charles is not providing her with the joys her readings had led her to expect. We are told in the last sentence of chapter 5: "And Emma sought to understand exactly what was meant in life by the words *felicity, passion* and *intoxication,* which had seemed so beautiful to her in books."

Emma's exaggerated hopes for her marriage could never be sat-isfied, but her frustration contains a distinct overtone of something more concrete: an absence of sexual satisfaction. The novel's scandal-ous reputation was founded on such overtones. Nineteenth-century bourgeois culture was not willing to pay such attention to female sex-uality. Flaubert need not be explicit here; the merest allusion suffices to give a bad conscience to a society that still wanted to think of its differences in terms of activity and passivity, masculinity and femininity.

This sexual allusion, however discrete, suffices to place Emma in a different sphere from her romantic counterparts. The language of romantic love is not without sexual connotations, but these are, to use a familiar Freudian term, "sublimated." We never ask whether the romantic heroine was sexually fulfilled, just as we do not ask how sexually explicit was Dante's desire for Beatrice. Romantic fulfillment is situated on a higher plane, where the reality of physical consummation, whether or not we may assume it to have occurred, is secondary. For we are speaking not of real acts but of cultural products, about which we can only learn what their creators considered significant. The adolescent readers of romantic novels, particularly the female ones, are not supposed to seek in their own lives specific experiences that correspond to "felicity" or "passion," any more than the reader of a fairy tale should expect to marry a prince. These literary works are meant to provide idealized models for experience, models that remain at a distance.

But Emma is too modern a character to respect this distance. She has already entered the age of the consumer, with none of the irony with which we have learned after a century to receive the claims of advertising. Rather than treating the heroines of her books as quasi-sacred figures, she treats them as examples of real-life possibilities. But this implies a physical literalism that struck the readers of Flaubert's time as something akin to blasphemy. Emma's dissatisfaction implies a *demystification* of the sublimity of romantic love, its reduction to tangible realities that she now finds inexplicably absent from her own life. Her attitude has already taken the decisive step toward the reduction of the spiritual to the material that would lead to Freud's doctrine of sexuality as the root of all desire.

The fifth chapter, which ends with the word "books," introduces the exploration of Emma's adolescent readings and religious experiences in the following chapter. The integration of religious and aesthetic experience was indeed characteristic of the romantic era, as typified by Chateaubriand's massive tome *Le Génie du christianisme* (*The Spirit of Christianity*), which the sisters had Emma's class read on Sundays "for recreation." In reaction to the rationalistic agnosticism of the *philosophes* that had led to the Revolution, early nineteenth-century conservatives saw religion as the bulwark of the social order. But in a century where the Self had begun to cultivate itself for the marketplace, religion had to be sold as a source less of eternal salvation than of immediate emotional and even sensual gratification.

Emma's adolescent experiences follow a well-defined pattern. The first sentence of the sixth chapter speaks of her as having read, before the onset of puberty, the late eighteenth-century sentimental classic *Paul et Virginie* (*Paul and Virginia*), which depicts the sexually ambiguous relationship of two adolescents brought up more or less as brother and sister—the cultural model for films like *The Blue Lagoon*. Then at thirteen, at the moment of entering the convent school, she reads on a set of painted dishes the story of Mme de La Vallière, a favorite of Louis XIV who became a nun at the age of thirty. During her first months in the convent, Emma is attracted to the aesthetic aspects of Christianity, but especially to the value it places on the denial of the senses:

> Instead of following the Mass, she examined in her book the pious azure-bordered vignettes, and she loved the sick lamb, the Sacred Heart pierced with sharp arrows, or poor Jesus who falls while carrying his cross. In order to mortify her flesh, she tried to go a whole day without eating. She searched in her mind for some vow to accomplish.

Emma turns away from the Mass's celebration of the mystery of communion to look at images of sacred victims. These figures may be counterpoised to the banal victimization of Charles on his first day at school; no such persecution is ever Emma's lot. The central position of the victim in the Christian ethos makes Emma yearn for sufferings of her own, whence her quasi-comical attempt at self-mortification. Emma has been taught to expect that the renunciation of earthly pleasures will give her life an infinitely greater significance than their satisfaction. In this naively perverse form of the "imitation of Christ," Emma seeks not salvation but self-importance. All this is not without sexual overtones of its own, as the next paragraph makes clear:

> When she went to confession, she invented little sins, in order to remain there longer, on her knees in the shadow, her hands together, her face at the grating under the whispering of the priest. The comparisons of betrothed, spouse, heavenly lover and eternal marriage

that recur in sermons aroused in the depths of her soul unexpected delights.

Here the masochism we encountered on our first meeting with Emma (her pricking and sucking her fingers while sewing) is given a spiritual basis. Emma invents sins in order to submit herself to the domination of the priest. The sexual connotation of this relationship is emphasized by the second sentence, which does not follow in chronological sequence. This passage is a good example of the psycho-analytic aspect of Flaubert's technique: he brings out the sexual un-dercurrents of the confessional by associating it with the sermons. We cannot know whether Emma herself made this association; the author merely juxtaposes the two mental images and lets us draw our own conclusions.

As an adolescent girl of a good family, Emma has no normal out-let for her awakening sexual desires. But it would be superficial to explain her religious sensibilities as simply displacements or sublima-tions of these desires. Emma must wait until marriage for sexual grat-ification; but in her religious reveries this very waiting is given a value. The real connection between the confessional and the sexual meta-phors of the sermon is not the person of the priest but the Christian emphasis on the link between renunciation and reward. Emma is not really renouncing anything, but by interpreting her life in these terms, she can imagine herself to be accumulating a kind of sexual capital that continually grows in value. Each "sin" makes Emma more pre-cious in her own eyes, more worthy of an imagined divine felicity. The "unexpected delights" are those associated with the delicious modern sensation of discovering one possesses a value one had not previously suspected. The more faithfully she humbles herself, the greater the re-ward she fancies is promised to her.

Emma's consumerism becomes more apparent in the following paragraph, which describes her reaction to her first readings of ro-mantic prose—that of Chateaubriand's *Spirit of Christianity*:

> How she listened, the first times, to the sonorous lamentation of
> romantic melancholies repeated by all the echoes of the earth and

of eternity! If her childhood had taken place in the back room of a shop in a commercial neighborhood, she would perhaps have opened up to the lyric effusions of nature, which ordinarily reach us only as translated by writers. But she knew the countryside too well; she was acquainted with the bleating of flocks, with dairies and ploughs. Accustomed to its calm aspects, she turned rather to its irregularities. She loved the sea only for its storms, and greenery only when it was scattered among ruins. She had to be able to derive from things a kind of personal profit; and she rejected as useless all that did not contribute to her heart's immediate consumption—being of a temperament more sentimental than artistic, seeking emotions and not landscapes.

The key to Emma's character is that she is "sentimental" rather than "artistic"; she seeks personal profit rather than aesthetic revelation. (Later in the chapter, Flaubert will call her a "positive spirit.") This passage describes Emma's moment of transition from religion to literature, or in more general cultural terms, from preromanticism to romanticism. Her longing for the "heavenly lover" remained bound to a traditional vocabulary and modes of action (prayer, confession). Emma's religious attitudes were romantic, but their forms of expression had remained classical—as the preromantic French poet André Chénier had advised the poets of his time to "make ancient verses about new ideas." Now Emma discovers a language that corresponds more specifically to her needs. These needs cannot adequately be described as merely emotional. Emma is touched by "romantic melancholies" because they provide a means of giving meaning to experience outside of the ritual context of the confessional.

Flaubert makes an important distinction between Emma and the more typical readers of this sort of prose. The city dweller will long for the beauties of nature; as a country girl, Emma knows "nature" all too well. This comparison of Emma with a child brought up "in the back room of a shop" masks a subtle distinction between Self and Other, male and female. Emma is not a full-fledged romantic Self like Frédéric Moreau, the protagonist of Flaubert's later novel, *Sentimental Education*. The city-dweller's idyllic vision of "nature" gives him a liberating distance from reality that Emma lacks. Her practical familiarity with the countryside deprives her of the ability to project onto nature, as Flaubert did in adolescent works like "Mémoires d'un fou," budding desires conceived within the world of family intimacy. But this only makes her romanticism all the more frenetic. Unlike the reader for whom nature serves as a guarantee of an underlying harmony between himself and the world, Emma can give value to her existence only by losing herself in the unknown. She requires a continuous flow of exotic visions for the "immediate consumption" of her imagination.

It is in this context that the adolescent Emma makes contact with secular literature. Significantly enough, she does not seek out these readings herself; an old seamstress from a ruined noble family brings the girls romantic novels to read. Emma follows the natural development of someone who "sought emotions and not landscapes." The amorous vocabulary that had first been evoked in a religious context is now fleshed out. Emma finds in literature not stories but images; models not of acts but of decors and attitudes.

Emma's transition from religious to literary experience substitutes the activity of her imagination for the real-world devotional activities of religion. Her childish attempts at ritual action—penance and fasting—give way to the consumption of literature. The sexual element that had been sublimated in her attraction to the submissive posture of the confessional and to dreams of a heavenly spouse is absorbed by literary imagery. By identifying with the heroines of her readings, Emma is able to give a specific value to her sexuality rather than making it a simple object of renunciation; her dreams contribute to the greater glory of herself rather than to that of God. The sort of self-valorization we saw in the confessional scene is insufficient because it requires implementation through real acts of "mortification" with respect to which Emma's timid gestures are inadequate. Religion asks of the individual what he or she can really give, and therefore does not lend itself to wholly imaginary satisfactions. In contrast, literature proposes its images within a fictional world; one "identifies" with them without it ever being a question of realizing them in practice.

In contrast to the adolescent in traditional society, for whom puberty constituted an abrupt transition from childish inactivity to mature action and a concomitant loss of innocence, the romantic adolescent acquires a new set of images through which she learns to live passively even after attaining biological maturity. Romantic religion of the kind preached by Chateaubriand is merely a transitory phase, an acting-out that cannot remain competitive with literature because it remains too closely bound to traditional practices to contribute to the adolescent's imaginary acquisition of self-value.

We should not forget that Flaubert is exploring desire as a quality not of the Self but of the Other. Emma's literary dreams, as has often been remarked, parallel the author's at her age. But young Gustave's literary efforts were dominated by an emotion that Emma only experiences in its most generalized form: his feeling of resentment toward his scholastically successful brother and through him toward his father as well. The adolescent Gustave's favorite figure was not a romantic hero but the Roman emperor Nero, whom he admired for his "aesthetic" cruelty. Emma's romantic adolescence is not so much an autobiographical reminiscence as an attempt to construct a character wholly molded by cultural factors, just as Saint Anthony's visions were the product less of Flaubert's imagination than of his studies. Emma is not led to romantic escapism to compensate for a sense of personal or even social inferiority. On the contrary, she is presented throughout the novel as a desirable woman—the only desirable female figure in the book. When, later on, the banality of provincial life begins to stifle her, reading will be of little use. Religion and literature are for Emma specifically adolescent activities that determine her expectations and desires for adult life.

Literature in this chapter is seasoned with the music of romances and the engravings in the books and "keepsakes" (albums) Emma reads. Indeed, Flaubert describes these images at greater length than the texts, which are for Emma exclusively sources of attitudes, of *scenes*. The series of literary illustrations begins with "a young man in a waistcoat who held in his arms a young woman in a white dress," and ends with a fantastic landscape containing an incoherent hodgepodge of romantic *topoi*: "palm trees, firs, tigers on the right, a lion on the left, Tartar minarets on the horizon, Roman ruins in the foreground . . . and with a great perpendicular ray of sunlight trembling in the water, where set off like white smudges on a steel-gray surface, here and there, swans are swimming."

In this final spectacle the swans replace the white-robed, victim-like female figure. What these images offer Emma are not so much models of behavior, even of imaginary behavior, as objects that she can "consume" by associating them directly with herself in her present state. In the final tableau, the swans add a note of melancholy through their traditional association with death, as in the expression "swan song." This landscape, devoid of human figures, offers Emma a meaningful locus into which she can insert herself, with the swans appearing as metaphors of her adolescent martyrdom.

Emma is shown throughout this chapter as learning to deal with life through *cultural* rather than worldly experience. Her adolescent sexuality gives her a potential value as an object of masculine desire that her culture allows her to capitalize. The ultimate result, however, is disillusionment, since the "positive" Emma becomes tired of continually redefining herself through the consumption of cultural images. Toward the end of her stay in the convent, she turns away from both religion and literature, although, soon after leaving, farm life makes her nostalgic for the convent.

It is in this period of her existence that she encounters Charles: "When Charles came to her home for the first time, she considered herself to be quite disillusioned, having nothing more to learn, incapable of any further feeling." This blasé attitude is not the result of any specific disappointment, but it is not entirely a sham. Emma's expectations for adult life have been raised by the imaginary value she has acquired through her reading, and adult life has not yet offered her the means of realizing this value. Marriage is the only possible step forward, but Emma's isolation in the countryside provides few opportunities; Charles is presumably her first and only suitor.

Here is the concluding paragraph of the chapter:

> But the anxiety of a new state, or perhaps the irritation caused by the presence of this man [Charles], had sufficed to make her

believe that she finally possessed that marvelous passion which until then had hovered like a great rosy-feathered bird in the splendor of poetic skies; and now she could not imagine that this calm in which she was living was the happiness of which she had dreamed.

Emma has just been described as someone "who had loved the church for its flowers, music for its words of romance, and literature for its sensual excitements." Cultural imagery offers the adolescent Emma immediate sensual gratification that is at the same time the anticipation of future bliss. For the image, even when "consumed," remains a sign of her renunciation of the reality it represents and thereby an emblem of her own value. The ultimate expression of her desire is therefore not the image of an ideal lover, but a figure of religious transcendence. The great bird Emma sees hovering overhead is an ancestor of the figure of the Holy Spirit in the form of a dove/parrot that would obsess the heroine of *A Simple Heart*.

The contrast between the calm of Emma's present reality and the transcendental "passion" she had hoped to possess does not imply that the real is necessarily inferior to the ideal, only that a more fevered reality would be a good thing, the opposite of "calm" being above all sexual excitement. The essence of Emma's desire is passive, but even at this stage of her life she does not passively accept the incompatibility between the banality of her life and the sublimity of her imagination. Emma has consumed imagery in preparation for being "consumed" as an object of male sexual desire. But the adolescent's inactivity makes it impossible to know whether the value she has accumulated for herself will ever be cashed in. As a preliminary answer to the question "What does the Other want?" this chapter suggests: to consume and be consumed at the same time.

The following (seventh) chapter recounts Emma's increasing discontentment with her marriage. One key to this dissatisfaction is the contrast between country and city life that is accentuated throughout the novel, beginning with the subtitle, "Moeurs de province" (a contemporary translation might be "Provincial Lifestyles"). Emma imagines her former schoolmates as having married more interesting men than Charles, but above all she envies their urban existence: "In the city, with the noise of the streets, the murmur of the theaters and the brightness of the balls, they had existences in which the heart expands, the senses bloom. But *her* life was as cold as an attic with its window facing north. . . ."

The real significance of the country/city opposition in *Madame Bovary* is not obvious at first sight. The immediate reaction of most readers of the novel is to identify with Emma's distaste for small-town life and to share her feeling that, had she lived in the city, particularly in Paris, her existence would have been less mediocre. Why indeed did Flaubert insist not only on writing about a woman, but about a provincial woman? His first novel, *Sentimental Education* (1845), had dealt with life in Paris.

Let us recall that in the world of *Madame Bovary* Emma is consistently portrayed as the only sexually attractive woman and never exposed to any kind of amorous rivalry. Her envy for her schoolmates remains on a general plane; throughout the novel, she never encounters anyone in particular to envy. This sets her apart from her milieu in a way that would be impossible in the city. Emma retains throughout her life the protective coating given by her adolescent dreams. Her sexual dissatisfaction, her sense of being out of her natural element are negative side effects of this indispensable insulation from competition that only provincial life can provide.

Similarly, the modern Self-as-consumer is never really in competition with others, because he or she never comes into direct contact with them; each is shielded by a subjective world nourished by the imagery of consumption. This situation does not prevent envy, but it tends to generalize it, or to focus it on the distant stars of the mass media. Thus the citizen of consumer society is essentially "provincial." Emma, as a prophetic model of the modern Self, must remain isolated from the models she envies. This isolation not only reinforces Emma's sense of superiority to her milieu; it contributes to her desirability. Emma always remains at the center of her provincial universe. *Madame Bovary* succeeds where its heroine fails because, even if the desires of her fictional lovers have their limits, Emma remains absolutely desirable to the reader.

Part 1

THE VAUBYESSARD BALL (CHAPTER 8)

As a consequence of his successful treatment of an abscess, Charles and his wife are invited to a ball given by a local marquis. This incident leaves its mark on Emma; it serves her as a demonstration that there indeed exists a better life than her own.

One of Flaubert's earliest preserved literary efforts describes a dance. For Flaubert, the dance is a quasi-sacred moment where one's individual choice of a sexual partner becomes part of a public ritual. It is not an orgy where one indulges one's desires one-sidedly, but a celebration of the harmony between desiring and being desired. For Emma, the Vaubyessard ball is a certification of her continuing desirability, a proof that she has not lost with marriage the sexual value she had accumulated at puberty. Here, as throughout the novel, Emma is not the jealous inferior to the other women. That she is included at all in this artistocratic milieu is a triumph for her. The fact that this inclusion is only temporary is no defeat, because it can be blamed on Charles's mediocre status. This visit certifies Emma's feeling of superiority to her own bourgeois environment and to her husband in particular.

It is easier for Emma than for Charles to become a part of the world of the ball. Neither knows how to waltz; but a man can show a woman the steps, whereas the opposite would be unlikely. Thus Charles sits on the sidelines while Emma dances away. Emma's temporary but real inclusion is emphasized from the beginning:

> Charles's buggy stopped before the central staircase; servants appeared; the marquis came forward, and, offering his arm to the doctor's wife, led her into the vestibule.

> The marquis opened the door of the parlor; one of the women rose (the marquise herself), went to greet Emma and had her sit beside her, on a love-seat, where she began to speak to her amiably, as though she had known her for a long time.

The marquis offers his arm to Emma; he opens the door to the couple, then the marquise invites Emma to sit beside her. We may doubt whether Charles received similar treatment; in any case the novel makes no mention of it. This is an effect of the "point-of-view" narration Flaubert uses in this episode. Because all is described through Emma's eyes, we only learn of what is of interest to her. Although the reader is able to judge what he sees for himself—for example, we understand that the marquise's familiarity is merely a form of impersonal politeness—he is never offered a means of experiencing the scene in a different way. What we can speak of as Emma's self-centeredness is forced on us by this technique. All experience is by definition subjective; but the subjective can appear either as a necessary component of a movement toward objectivity, or as a reality closed upon itself. The point-of-view technique, which in its mature form Flaubert may be said to have invented, sets the reader before the world of his heroine's subjective impressions, forces us to share her experience *aesthetically*. We are never able to attribute to Emma the exercise of an objective judgment on these impressions, for in the absence of the traditional narrator-figure, there is no objective perspective from which the impressions may be judged:

> Emma felt herself, on entering [the dining room], enveloped in a warm atmosphere, a mixture of the scent of the flowers and of the fine linen, of the aroma of the meats and the odor of the truffles. The candles in the chandeliers spread their flames over the silver dish-covers; the pieces of cut crystal, covered with a dull mist, reflected each others' pale gleams; there were bouquets of flowers lined up along the whole length of the table, and, in the wide-rimmed plates, the napkins, arranged like bishop's miters, each held in the opening of their folds an oval roll. The lobsters' red claws stuck out of the serving-dishes; large pieces of fruit in open-work baskets were piled upon moss; the quails still had their feathers, fumes rose in the air. . . . On the large porcelain stove with copper rods, the statue of a woman draped up to her chin stared motionless at the room full of people.

This passage is an excellent illustration of Flaubert's descriptive technique. Beginning with the sensation of his central character ("Emma felt . . . "), he presents the scene as a series of *phenomena*, of distinct experiences of a world of objects. The atmosphere that envelops Emma at the beginning of the passage is built up for the reader, whose imaginary experience of the scene gradually becomes indistinguishable from Emma's own. This experience is deliberately impressionistic; it is not the product of a restructuring of reality into rational categories: food, drink, tableware, decor. But Flaubert's description possesses an order of a different kind.

Let us examine more closely the second sentence of the paragraph. First we see the flames of the candles reflected from the silver dish covers; then the dull reflections of the crystal; then the flowers, which give off no light of their own, and finally the napkins on the plates. The visual objects are arranged in order of decreasing brilliance and increasing banality, until we reach the plates of the individual diners. The bizarre conjunction of the bishop's miter and the roll, a kind of bourgeois Communion-wafer, is never affirmed as anything more than a *formal* association; the napkins are "arranged like" miters, the rolls "oval in shape" (*de forme ovale*). From the rolls we go on to the food itself; the lobsters' claws and the fruit, the quails, and the rising fumes, which bring us back to the aromas evoked at the beginning of the passage. But by now it is no longer Emma but the reader who is enveloped in them.

The bright visual images are the easiest to imagine, the most "objective." These relatively abstract signs of wealth (crystal and silver—in French this word also means "money") precede the abundance of goods for immediate consumption (lobsters, fruit), with the "bishops" offering their rolls in between. The passage from the candles to the rolls and to the food does not follow the logic of a series of acts; it is not a true narrative sequence. We may attribute its organization to the movement of Emma's attention, but in any case it dictates the movement of our own attention. All the objects of this description are perfectly plausible; Flaubert had no doubt observed them at countless dinner parties. But by referring to them he makes them something other than subordinate elements of the general action of serving dinner to one's guests. Whether or not we attribute the comparison between the napkins and miters to Emma, it creates a connotation that goes beyond the functional presentation of objective reality.

The napkins have been placed on the plates as part of the hosts' offering of a meal to their guests; but for Emma they are signs of communion with a higher, an inaccessible world. Her hosts' use of them involves no emotional investment or even any particular attention. But Emma at the Vaubyessard mansion is not engaging in social relations, but consuming sensations. Her experience is not that of a participant in human interaction but of an observer fascinated by the trappings of this interaction. Emma inhabits a world where the significance of human relations in themselves has been taken over by the objects that accompany them. In the context of a formal dinner, what matters is not the food itself, nourishment for the body, but the accompanying connotations of paradisal plenty and grace.

The final sentence adds a bit of sociological irony. The fully draped statue that "stares motionless" at the crowd reflects the aristocracy's conformity to the bourgeois prudery of the nineteenth century; one imagines that before the Revolution the statue would have been nude. The statue's stare is reminiscent of that of the monsters in the *Temptation*. Like the bishop's miters, it suggests a degraded sacrality; the miters consecrate the "daily bread" of a vulgarized Christianity, while this nameless nymph or goddess looks down impotently on a society that no longer worships at her altar. All this is merely suggested; unlike Balzac, Flaubert never makes explicit points of sociological analysis. The blank absurdity of his vision of the social universe is suggested, here as in many other places in the novel, by an object whose presence in the scene is so little motivated that the emptiness of its message can be experienced without being interpreted. In this way, Flaubert presents his reader with a text that "shows" without "telling," that is, "authored" rather than narrated.

But the dinner is only the preliminary to the ball. In this privileged moment, the immediate physical contact of human beings provides a more immediate guarantee of the symbolic significance of the objects on the dinner table. No real relationships are established, but images of possible relationships are stored up for future use:

> At three in the morning, the cotillion began. Emma did not know how to waltz. Everyone was waltzing. . . .

But one of the waltzers who was called familiarly *the Viscount*, whose wide open waistcoat seemed molded to his chest, came for a second time to invite Mme Bovary, assuring her that he would guide her and that she would do quite well.

They began slowly, then went faster. They turned: everything turned around them, the lamps, the furniture, the walls, and the floor, like a disk on a pivot. Passing near the doors, Emma's dress, from below, caught against his trousers, their legs intertwined, he lowered his eyes to her, she lifted hers to him; a torpor came over her, she stopped. They took off again; and, with a more rapid movement, the Viscount, drawing her along, disappeared with her to the end of the gallery, where, out of breath, she nearly fell, and, for an instant, leaned her head on his chest. And then, still turning, but more slowly, he led her back to her seat; she sank back against the wall and put her hand before her eyes.

Here Emma, the outsider, is again made the object of a special choice, this time of a more explicitly sexual character. The Viscount, a paragon of aristocratic grace, comes twice to invite Emma to dance with him. The dance scene is constructed like a simulation of sexual intercourse. Emma at first becomes dizzy, then physical contact is made, then she obtains a kind of languorous reciprocity as her eyes meet those of her partner. Giving herself over to a delicious passivity, she loses control over her movements, as the Viscount "disappears" with her over the horizon . . . or at least to the end of the dance floor. This is the stuff utopias are made of.

There is a subtle interplay between objective and subjective description. A phrase like "everything turned around them" makes a pretense of objectivity, while evidently describing the scene from Emma's perspective—one hardly imagines that the Viscount experiences it in these terms. The text increasingly emphasizes the reciprocity of the two partners: their legs intertwine (literally "entered into one another"); finally, the look they exchange is described in parallel clauses: "he lowered his eyes to her, she lifted hers to him." The relationship is both reciprocal and hierarchical; the man and the woman play parallel roles, but one is clearly dependent on the other. Emma does not seek strict equality: it is appropriate that the man should look down from above, the woman up from below. In this acceptance of sexual subordination, the reality of social subordination is momentarily forgotten. The Viscount no longer appears to inhabit a different world; they are merely a man and a woman. Emma has at last found a model for the realization of her sexual value, a proof that this value transcends social differences. For the rest of her life, she will reproach Charles with his inability to achieve the fusion of social superiority with sexual dominance that she found momentarily in the Viscount's arms.

It is thus precisely at the moment where the description appears the most objective that it is the least so. The Viscount is not even passingly interested in Emma; he simply enjoys dancing. The reciprocity of the dance is not a physical reality but a psychological illusion that the author's language "objectively" allows us, like Emma, to entertain. At the end of this utopian sentence, a torpor comes over her, a state of euphoria that precludes any further desire. Emma has attained through the ceremony of the dance the harmony between desiring and being desired that she will never be able to obtain in real life.

Later, on the way home, Emma sees the Viscount pass on the road, and on stopping to fix their carriage, Charles finds a cigar case he has dropped. On attempting to smoke one of the cigars, Charles becomes sick; Emma grabs the case and saves it as a relic. The symbolism of all this is painfully clear. In Rouen shortly before her suicide, Emma will fancy she sees the Viscount pass by in his carriage, a fleeting figure of illusory hope.

The Vaubyessard ball is a turning point in the story. From this time on, Emma no longer merely wonders why marriage has not brought her happiness; she is convinced that a better world exists, and that her alliance with Charles can be blamed for her exclusion from it.

Emma's search for a utopia of sexual submissiveness is not the expression of a woman's yearning, but a male experiment in imagining experience from the Other's perspective. The same Flaubert who wrote at fifteen of the rapture of the dance now witnesses this rapture from the opposite point of view, one which reveals the hollowness of its

ceremonial promise of harmonious desire. A world emptied of its traditional values can no longer incarnate the desires of a Self; it can only
be seen through an Other's eyes. What Emma finds at the Vaubyessard
ball is not the object of her desire, but the image of her desirability.
The Viscount's gestures merely furnish points of departure for Emma's
mental imagery. As we saw in our discussion of free indirect discourse,
this imagery is neither true nor false; imaginary satisfaction is more
fundamental than truth.

The aristocratic ambience of the Vaubyessard château gives evidence of the transformation of historic tradition into a mere set of
images. The initial description of the château as "of modern construction, in the Italian style," the reduction of the portraits in the family
gallery to a set of disembodied highlights, the prudishly covered statue
who stares at the diners are so many indications that the nobility has
been reduced to a set of empty yet prestigious signs within bourgeois
society. Flaubert, who was a more uncompromising critic of this society than were the romantics, recognized in it a trend that would only
become apparent in our era. His constant insistence on the priority of
consumption over production is based on his intuition that it is the
former, not the latter, which has become the motive force in social
relations. Fifty years before Proust, Flaubert understood that the role
of the old nobility in the bourgeois world is to provide marketable
signs of historical permanence. The bourgeois romantic fancies himself the possessor of an aristocratic value that stands above the market; Emma receives from the Viscount the assurance of her own
absolute worth.

12

Part 2

The Bovarys Arrive in Yonville (Chapters 1–2)

Yonville-l'Abbaye is the locus of the main action of the novel, and Flaubert sets the stage carefully with four pages of description. The landscape is first characterized rather lyrically as resembling "a great outspread coat with a velvet collar bordered with silver braid." But as if to assure the reader, or himself, that so positive a tone cannot be maintained, a few lines further on the description becomes bitingly satirical:

> We are here on the frontiers of Normandy, Picardy and the Ile-de-France, a bastard region where the language is without accentuation, as the landscape is without character. It is here that they make the worst Neufchâtel cheeses in the whole district. . . .

How can a landscape that resembles a "great outspread coat" be "without character"? One senses that the author's power over his text is being exercised tyrannically, through "telling" rather than "showing." The cheeses are not part of the narrative; they are a gratuitous means for discrediting Yonville. This Normandy town must be shown as possessing the disadvantages of provincial life without its compensating regional charm. The setting for this tale must lack any values of its own; it must be cut off from all contact with social creativity, a world as secondhand as Emma's desires.

The description continues by mocking the lack of economic acumen of the inhabitants, who fail to take advantage of the new road that passes through it—although they are later described as relatively well-off. The church, newly rebuilt, is beginning to deteriorate; its chief decoration is described (in italics) as a painting of "the *Holy Family, donation of the Minister of the Interior.*" The Interior Ministry is concerned above all with police functions; its gift signifies the cooptation of religion by what the French call "the forces of order." This reflection is no doubt more appropriate to the regime of Napoleon III under which the novel was written than to Louis-Philippe's monarchy during which the action takes place.

To conclude these introductory remarks. Flaubert assures the reader that "since the events that we are about to recount, nothing, in fact, has changed in Yonville. . . ." Rather than claiming for his narrative any kind of collective importance, Flaubert insists on its uneventful nature, just as the schoolboy narrator of the first pages had insisted that no one would be able to remember anything about Charles. The very indifference of the town to the Bovarys' downfall renders their story not less but more significant, the permanence of bourgeois society being founded on its indifference to matters of real human concern. The Second Empire's disregard of the democratic ideals of 1848 seemed to the writers of the era to justify the notion of a permanent opposition between the social and the human.

The passage continues:

> The tin tricolor flag still turns on top of the church steeple; the draper's shop still waves in the wind its two calico streamers; the pharmacist's fetuses, like bundles of white tinder, disintegrate more and more in their muddy alcohol, and, above the front door of the inn, the old golden lion, faded by the rain, still displays to the passers-by its poodle's mane.

All the important locales of Yonville are mentioned in this passage: the inn where the inhabitants congregate, the church where Emma will fail to find religious consolation, the draper's shop that will drain her financial resources, Homais's pharmacy. . . . There is a distinctively Flaubertian quality in the choice of objects to express continuity. The flag, signifying the permanence of the alliance between church and state, and the streamers that draw attention to Lheureux's wares are public objects, and their continuity is expressed by immediately visible movements (turning, waving). Both these symbols are "modern": Flaubert chooses not traditional religion and agriculture, but "the forces of order" and the consumer market. In contrast, the fact that the fetuses, the only trace of life in this scene, are rotting "more and more" could only be observed from a historical perspective. Life in Yonville is neither renewed nor permanent; it is something preserved from the past that slowly dissolves, like the traditional Self in the modern world. The superficial observer sees the "modern" flag and streamers, a more penetrating eye senses the decay; Flaubert's narrator is both and neither of these figures. The inn's weatherbeaten "golden lion" survives as a sign of tradition, but this old symbol has never had more nobility or fierceness than a poodle.

All the major figures of the village appear at the inn to welcome the Bovarys: the pharmacist Homais; Bournisien, the local priest; Binet, the tax-collector who spends his free time making napkin-rings; and young Léon, who will later become Emma's second lover.

On their arrival, the Bovarys sit down to dinner with Homais and Léon and engage in the first extended conversation of the novel. As the French critic Jean-Pierre Richard has observed, a great deal of eating takes place in Flaubert's works. Just as the dance was for Flaubert the most intense form of secular ritual, the dinner is the most typical. The interplay of different dinner-table conversations makes all of them appear inconsequential. While Homais regales Charles with pompous gossip, Léon and Emma exchange romantic clichés. This is the first time that Emma has found a kindred soul with whom to share her yearnings. Their dialogue is a notable demonstration of the kind of exchange that is facilitated by the romantic cultural vocabulary:

> [Léon:] Sometimes, on Sundays, I go [to the top of a hill] and I stay there with a book, watching the sunset.
> [Emma:] I can think of nothing more admirable than sunsets, she replied, but especially at the seashore.
> —Oh! I adore the sea, said M. Léon.
> —And then, doesn't it seem to you, replied Mme Bovary, that the spirit sails more freely on that limitless expanse, that to look upon it uplifts your soul and gives you ideas of the infinite, of the ideal?

In this passage Emma and Léon share their secondhand experiences. Emma has presumably never seen the sea, yet she knows from her reading, not that the sea is beautiful or magnificent, but that it is appropriate to say so. This experience can be shared all the more easily because it is purely cultural. Such communication conveys no information; it is a communion between two selves who recognize and appreciate each other's "uniqueness." The experiences they share are solitary; the superior soul has no direct contact with others, only with nature at its most magnificent. But this refusal of the social is precisely what allows the couple to exchange signs of uniqueness without entering into competition with each other. Neither needs to prove he or she is the more truly unique; both are set off from the society of common mortals presumably too preoccupied with mundane pursuits ever to admire the sunset or the sea. These objects of literary adoration are conventional, but there is a world of difference between convention and tradition. The whole point of admiring the sunset is that it is presumed *not* to be a traditional object of admiration, not to have been previously assimilated by the culture. The sunset is a natural phenomenon that presumably appeals to us directly, without the mediation of our apprenticeship in the ways of society. The romantic cliché is all the more devastating because it pretends to be just the opposite of a cliché.

This passage exemplifies Flaubert's subversive approach to dialogue. The author need make no commentaries, and the characters' words themselves need not be, like those of Homais, excessive or ridiculous. The more they parrot what Flaubert called "received ideas," the more they display not merely their own unoriginality but the impossibility of any worldly originality. Flaubert demonstrates in *Madame Bovary* that no depiction of worldly experience can make it appear unique; it can only be described in its own language, which is that of cliché. But the author, unlike his characters and the books they have read, makes no pretense of palming off the cliché on us as something truly original.

Here is a later phase of the same dialogue:

> [Léon:] . . . what could be better, indeed, than to sit in the evening at one's fireside with a book, while the wind strikes the window-panes, and the lamp burns? . . .
>
> —How true, she said, staring at him with her great black eyes wide open.
>
> —You think of nothing, he continued, the hours pass. You are walking, motionless, through countries you think you see, and your mind, embracing the fiction, amuses itself with the details or follows the line of the plot. It becomes absorbed in the characters; it seems to be you who are throbbing beneath their costumes.
>
> —That's true! that's true! she said.
>
> —Has it ever happened to you, Léon continued, to come across in a book a vague idea you have had, some obscure image that returns from far away, more or less the full expression of your most delicate feeling?
>
> —I have felt that, she answered.
>
> —That is why, he said, I love the poets above all. I find verse more tender than prose, and it makes you cry far better.
>
> —But it becomes tiresome in the end, replied Emma; and now, on the contrary, I adore tales that never stop for breath, where you are afraid. I hate commonplace heroes and moderate feelings, such as there are in nature.
>
> —Indeed, observed the clerk, since those works don't touch the heart, they stray, it seems to me, from the true purpose of Art.

This second passage is more personal: now Emma and Léon share their actual experiences of reading, not the fictional ones they find in their books. Here there is room for argument; Emma disagrees with her interlocutor's choice of literary genre. Léon describes the joys of identification with fictional characters. Like seas and sunsets, books are objects of solitary experience, but on a secondary level. Yet the vicarious experience of books is more real for Emma and Léon than that of the real world. It is here that they encounter the representations that make the sea and the sunset worth talking about. And both have experienced the special thrill of finding in a book their own intimate reflections, discovering that in their anonymous lives they may still have thoughts of general significance.

This attitude toward reading did not exist before the nineteenth century. For the first time in history, large numbers of people had become educated just enough to appreciate the fact that they were "out of it," that their thoughts and feelings were no longer guaranteed of acceptance within their cultural tradition. This is a feeling familiar to us, but not to the members of traditional societies. The romantic self continually demands reassurance from the surrounding culture as to the marketability of its sentiments.

That Léon enjoys tender poetry "that makes you cry better" whereas Emma is more drawn to what we would today call thrillers is, on the most obvious level, a foretaste of the reversal of masculine and feminine roles that will later occur in their love relationship. But more importantly, this inversion illustrates the change in emphasis pointed out by the Italian critic Mario Praz between the "fatal man" of the romantic era and the postromantic femme fatale. Léon prefers to cry while Emma prefers to experience terror; having less need to preserve her self-control, she is more willing than he to experience vicarious violence. For the woman is superior to the man in the experience of Otherness. She equates desire with being desired, and has no reason to feel a "tender" complacency toward a self that, as she realizes better than her masculine counterpart, has no autonomous existence of its own. What Emma wants is to be carried away from herself, not drawn into herself.

But their disagreement is not profound. They can agree that the point of Art is to touch "the heart." Emma's rejection of moderate sentiments "such as there are in nature" makes an interesting contrast with her admiration for the natural phenomena described earlier. She might, after all, have said, "as there are in real life." Flaubert emphasizes the ambiguity of the romantic notion of nature. Sunsets and seashores are not unusual phenomena, but they are presumably unusual *experiences,* reserved for unique souls. Here "nature" is opposed to "society," as the locus for feelings that do not depend on others. On the other hand, the "nature" Emma abhors is the world where things are as expected, where there is no thrill of sublime difference, the nature that as a farm girl she knows too well to dream about. It is thrilling to find one's private thoughts expressed in print because one is reassured of one's participation in the culturally significant; but it is unpleasant to find in books examples of one's everyday experiences, because one then suspects that the author is as far from the sublime as his readers.

THE AGRICULTURAL FAIR (CHAPTER 8)

The Fair episode is the turning point of the action of the novel, the moment at which Emma becomes ready to take the step beyond marital dissatisfaction to actual infidelity. It is also Flaubert's most daring scene from a technical standpoint. Like the Vaubyessard ball, the Fair is a collective ceremony, but rather than providing Emma with a vision of a better world, it fuels her sense of superiority to her own world's bourgeois vulgarity.

Emma becomes attached to Léon, but the relationship remains platonic, neither daring to conceive of an active love affair. Frustrated with life in Yonville and with lack of progress in his relations with Emma, Léon finally goes off to Paris to study. Emma reacts by spending money on caprices and aborted projects. It is at this moment of boredom and quiet despair that Rodolphe enters the scene. One look at Emma suffices to show him that she is ripe for seduction. He exclaims to himself: "Poor little woman! It's gasping for love like a carp for water on a kitchen table."

Part 2

The Fair is a major event in Yonville, a display of public vanity and an occasion for political discourses. Rodolphe's strategy of seduction uses the public event as a backdrop for the private; collective activity becomes a means to intensify the intimacy of his dialogue with Emma. As they visit the exhibits together, he speaks of his melancholy isolation:

> ... how many times, at the sight of a graveyard, in the moonlight, have I wondered if I wouldn't do better to join those who are sleeping there. . . .
> —Oh! And your friends? she said. You don't think of them.
> —My friends? But what friends? Do I have any? Who cares about me?

Rodolphe's conversation turns to his own ends the clichés that Léon and Emma had naively shared. By pretending to be alone in the world, he encourages Emma to see herself as playing a central role in his life. The romantic procedure of building up the Self by emphasizing its difference from others becomes here no longer a means of making contact but a technique of seduction. Preromantic Don Juans claimed not very credibly that their love was so intense that they could no longer live without their beloved. Rodolphe's technique is more sophisticated: he affirms that he has from the outset nothing in common with the world, no desire to go on living; Emma is drawn to participate in the seduction process by making the essential assumption that she alone can cure him of these somber thoughts.

Both before and after marriage, Emma has always acted in such a way as to maintain her "market value" as an object of desire. Her expenses on dresses and hairdos are signs of this; at their first meeting Rodolphe finds her "turned out like a Parisienne." She expected that with marriage this value would be converted into sexual and social fulfillment, but she soon discovered the contrary. This is only superficially the result of Charles's limitations. The world offers no means of translating the value accumulated through Emma's subjective adolescent self-sacrifice into objective satisfaction. Thus even after marriage and childbirth Emma remains fixed in the naive attitude of the adolescent who "mortified her flesh" in anticipation of unknown joys to come. Rodolphe exploits this situation by offering her a means of conceiving the bestowal of her favors as yet another sacrifice, this time with the purpose of saving a fellow being from mortal melancholy. In Emma's exchange with Léon, the two spoke of the exaltation that comes from the sense of one's separation from the world. Rodolphe makes use of the negative moment of romanticism, far more powerful in its rhetoric. Getting a good cry from his reading is not sufficient for him; he exploits its content as a means to the satisfaction of worldly appetites.

Rodolphe draws Emma away from the crowd, to a room in the empty courthouse overlooking the square where the Fair is being held. This allows him to play on the contrast between the couple's role as spectators of a public festivity and the intimate world of their conversation. The vapid political discourse of a government official, named rather pointedly Lieuvain, or "empty place"—a play on the term "lieu commun" or "commonplace," a synonym of "cliché"—mingles with Rodolphe's more personal politics. This technique is a radical extension of that employed in the conversation in the inn, when Homais's pseudoscientific gossip was played off against Emma's and Léon's exchange of romantic banalities. The present passage is more daringly authorial: the speakers are not in the same place and the alternation of their words cannot be said either to follow a strictly chronological order or to correspond to the perception of the event from any conceivable vantage point.

Varying the rhythm of his shifts back and forth from one scene to the other, Flaubert gradually intensifies the intermingling of the two sets of discourses. The partial attention of the couple to the scene below provides the pretext for the implementation of a new concept of the novelist's role in his narrative. All narration requires the storyteller to regulate the arrangement of the elements of his story, switching from one scene to another independently of strict chronology; this degree of control is already present in Homer's epics. But in the past each scene had always been perceived from a single point of view that might change as the scene progressed, but never shift abruptly back and forth. To use the analogy of film, earlier narratives had employed the techniques of traveling and zoom, with the author passing at will from one scene to another, or leaving the objective stance of an outside observer to enter into the consciousness of one of his characters. Flaubert was the first to use what is in effect a split screen that shows the intimate and the public worlds at the same time, and demonstrates the hollowness of both by unmasking their pretended independence of each other.

Flaubert never puts his authorial technique on display in *Madame Bovary*. His point is not to demonstrate his ability to conceive of technical innovations, but to accomplish a subtle subversion of the reader's expectations. Here the fact that Emma and Rodolphe are in a tenuous way still "attending" the Fair and listening to the speeches lends to his narrative a deceptive air of plausibility. Meanwhile the traditional narrative persona has been stripped of all its personal qualities; in this scene, it functions as no more than a tape recorder, or a "copyist," like Flaubert's last heroes, Bouvard and Pécuchet. As the rapidity of the alternation between the Fair and the couple intensifies, the reader becomes increasingly obliged to attribute the text to a mind that stands outside the scene. Flaubert not only reveals the equal triviality of the two types of discourse he juxtaposes, but he forces his reader to acknowledge that the only authentic understanding of the world he describes must be obtained from without. No traditional narrator, however omniscient, could make sense of a world in which all discourse is merely the repetition of anonymous commonplaces.

The climax of the scene follows the end of Lieuvain's speech. The chairman of the panel of judges begins to award prizes to the local farmers as Rodolphe intensifies his efforts:

> —We, now, he said, why have we met? What fatality willed it? It must have been that, from afar, no doubt, like two rivers whose flow brings them together, our individual inclinations had driven us toward each other.
> And he grasped her hand; she did not withdraw it.
> "Best overall farming!" cried the chairman.

—Just now, for example, when I came to your house . . .
"To M. Bizet, of Quincampoix."
—Did I know I would accompany you?
"Seventy francs!"
—A hundred times, in fact, I wanted to leave, and I followed you,
I remained.
"Manure."
—As I would remain tonight, tomorrow, every day, all my life!
"To M. Caron, of Argueil, a gold medal!"
—For never have I found in anyone's company so total a charm.
"To M. Bain, of Givry–Saint–Martin!"
—So as for me, I will cherish your memory.
"For a merino ram . . ."
—But you will forget me, I will have passed by like a shadow.
"To Mr. Belot, of Notre–Dame . . ."
—Oh! no, isn't it so that I will count for something in your
thought, in your life?
"Hogs, two equal prizes: to MM Lehérissé and Cullembourg;
sixty francs!"
Rodolphe squeezed her hand, and he felt it all warm and trem-
bling like a captive turtle-dove that wants to resume its flight; but,
whether she was trying to pull her hand away or responding to his
pressure, she moved her fingers; he cried:
—Oh! thank you! You do not repulse me! You are good! You
understand that I am yours! Let me see you, let me look at you!

This extraordinary passage merits careful analysis. There is no
pretense here, as there might have been earlier, that Rodolphe and
Emma are listening to the speech that rises from below like a commentary on theirs. Now the nature of this speech has changed: it is no
longer a tissue of political clichés designed to mask the cynical reality
of power, but a series of symbolic gifts from the public treasury. The
empty flow of rhetoric is replaced by the language of substantive, although derisory, events. The farmers are no longer being told in general terms how important they are; real money is being distributed.
Similarly, Rodolphe's rhetoric is now reaching its payoff. His seduction of Emma, as though responding to the encouragements of M.

Lieuvain, has attained the harvest stage. The rhythm of the awards now parallels, now punctuates that of the lover's declarations; the sentences are sometimes the same length, sometimes shorter, but never longer. The series of prizes involves a passage from inanimate to animate objects; from general farming to manure, to two hogs that tie for first prize. The latter offer a burlesque parallel with the couple who, despite the apparent difference of their roles, may be said to be equally wallowing in sensuality.

If Flaubert's narrative constantly foils the reader's attempts to construct the imaginary figure of a storyteller, in this scene the attempt must be renounced altogether. But our sense of being under the control of the extraworldly author does not inspire a feeling of security, of being in the hands of a higher power. On the contrary, authorial narrative inspires a feeling of abandonment. The "impassive" author who stands outside the world of the characters never directly expresses an *understanding* of it; he merely shows us a series of phenomena and lets us grasp its coincidences for ourselves. No narrator points out to us the parallel between Emma and Rodolphe on the one hand and a pair of prize hogs on the other. We are left to draw our own conclusions. If in this case the similarity seems rather obvious. it is more problematic in other cases. Are we to make anything of the names of the prize-winners? Is the ram a "symbol" of Rodolphe? Is "manure" to be taken as a commentary on Rodolphe's insincerity, or a suggestion that he is "fertilizing" the field of his conquest? Or should we imagine the whole scene as taking place in the field of Emma's consciousness, as sentence fragments from below blend with Rodolphe's more insistent words? Flaubert's refusal to offer the reader an imaginary figure to guide him through the world of the novel like Virgil and Beatrice through the circles of the *Divine Comedy* struck his original readers as disconcerting and even immoral, just as his appeal to today's "postmodern" readers is founded on this refusal.

Until this point in the novel, Emma, however disillusioned by her marriage and unsatisfied with her lot in life, has done nothing to overstep the bounds of respectability. Her chaste flirtation with Léon had been a continuation of the "sacrifices" of sensual satisfaction that she had earlier learned to make at the convent school. But *Madame Bovary* is not the story of a purely subjective revolt against the limitations of reality; it is a tale of the impossibility of reconciling desire with the world, even when one is willing to take risks to do so. This passage marks the beginning of Emma's transformation from a frustrated housewife to an adulteress.

There is a connection between the passage's radical technique and its central place in the story line. Flaubert is most present as author and least as narrator at the very moment at which both the opposition and the complicity between the romantic and the realistic, the intimate and the public, reach their high point. In the scene at the inn, Emma and Léon had shared a sense of superior refinement, of contempt for whatever is "in nature," but they had not thought for a moment to contrast their conversation with the platitudes that Homais was spouting at the very same table. They had referred to their noble loneliness, but they did not speak of their relationship as a unique asylum from a friendless world in which death may appear preferable to life. But at the same time, there was no suggestion that Homais's banalities were an ironic debunking of their talk. On the contrary, when Homais butts into their tête-à-tête, it is rather his own pedestrian insensitivity that is emphasized. Here, with the couple set off in a superior position, seeing but unseen, above the crowd at the Fair, with Rodolphe constantly emphasizing the gulf between the two noble souls and the "imbeciles" below, the platitudes of the officials turn Rodolphe's fine words to ridicule in the eyes of the reader.

The achievement of Flaubert's authorial tour de force in this passage is to demonstrate that separation and similarity are really indistinguishable; the further one pretends to be from the crowd, the more one resembles it. The narrator disappears altogether because there is no longer even the semblance of a common universe for him to inhabit. The two discourses seem to belong to separate worlds; yet both speak of distinction, that of the chosen souls at the window and that of the successful farmers below. For there exist in the modern world a multitude of discourses providing distinction to different, mutually exclusive groups of people, and although these discourses sound very different from one another, they are in essence the same, which is to say, equally false. Flaubert shows us that there are no real differences, and no neutral language of truth in which to express them. There are only the specialized languages the author must borrow in order to let the story tell itself.

But the lesson of the scene as far as Emma is concerned is that such a universe, however decked out in the trappings of morality, imposes no limits whatever on action. As Rodolphe tells her, "there are two moralities. . . . The petty . . . busies itself below, like that assemblage of imbeciles that you see. But the other, the eternal, is all around and above, like the landscape that surrounds us and the blue sky that lights our way." Which is only to say that there is no morality at all, that there is a language to justify any action, bourgeois rapaciousness as well as sexual irregularity. If Flaubert was put on trial for having published this novel, it was ultimately for his implied acceptance of this principle. Rodolphe's little trick of interpreting as a sign of consent Emma's movement of her hand, presumably in a half-hearted attempt to remove it, gives this lesson its ultimate point. If any sign may be interpreted in the sense most favorable to one's interests, then there are no symbolic or cultural forces capable of imposing restraints on one's actions. The Self-as-Other can pass from the stage of brandishing the Ideal as a compensation for reality to that of using it to justify the satisfaction of its worldly appetites.

Until now, Emma has clothed her life in romantic rhetoric, but only in the traditional sense that allows culture, as a more adaptable modern substitute for religion, to provide consolation for the world's failure to deliver the goods that would satisfy the desires it engenders. Now she is ready to take the decisive step into a more modern, as well as a more dangerous, world, where not traditional forces but market values are the only sources of restraint. Emma will not be brought down by her adulterous affairs, but by her financial extravagance. Sex is a free good; it is only when her supply of credit runs out that she will be forced to face disgrace and suicide. This too is prefigured in this passage, where the "reward" Emma is about to bestow on her lover finds an ironic parallel in the petty sums of money being doled out in the square below.

EMMA IN LOVE (CHAPTER 12)

After succumbing to Rodolphe's advances, Emma abandons herself wholeheartedly to their affair. When Rodolphe becomes less attentive, their relationship cools, and Emma makes a final attempt at reinvesting her affection in her marriage. But after poor Charles's disastrous attempt at repairing the village stableboy's club foot—an operation that she had hoped would bring glory to them both—Emma returns to Rodolphe with a vengeance. Her insistence that he run away from Yonville with her will shortly put an end to their liaison. The following passage, one of the few in the novel where Emma's own speech is presented at length, also contains one of Flaubert's most celebrated reflections on language:

> [Emma:] "I sometimes have such longings to see you again that all the furies of love tear me apart. I wonder: 'Where is he? Perhaps he is speaking to other women? They smile at him, he comes near...' Oh! no, it isn't so, none of them attract you? There are women more beautiful than I, but I know how to love better! I am your slave and your concubine! you are my king, my idol! you are good! you are handsome! you are intelligent! you are strong!"
>
> He had so often heard these things said to him that they held nothing original for him. Emma was like all mistresses; and the charm of novelty, gradually slipping off like a garment, displayed in its naked reality the eternal monotony of passion, which has always the same forms and the same language. He did not distinguish, this man so full of practical experience, the dissimilarity of feelings beneath the similarity of expressions. Because libertine or venal lips had murmured to him analogous phrases, he believed only weakly in the sincerity of these; you had to take them with a grain of salt, he thought, since exaggerated discourses hide mediocre affections; as if the fullness of the soul did not sometimes overflow into the most empty metaphors, since no one, ever, can give the exact measure of his needs, nor of his ideas, nor of his sufferings, and human language is like a cracked pot on which we beat tunes to a dancing bear, when we would like to melt the stars.

From what we know of Emma, her intemperate language strikes us as expressing less the depth of her affection than her pathological need to have her lover play the role of "king" and "idol" in her fantasies. Yet Flaubert reproaches Rodolphe with his inability to appreciate the sincerity or "candor" (the French word *candeur* is somewhere in between) of Emma's passion, in contrast to the less noble feelings of the sort of women he habitually frequented. This rejection of the superficial wisdom that thinks it can judge reality by discounting its rhetoric inspires the metaphor of language as a "cracked pot" (the French word *chaudron* is a familiar metaphor for an inferior musical instrument).

The author's spirited defense of his heroine is at first glance precisely the sort of editorial intervention that Flaubert was supposed to have banished from the novel. No doubt Emma is indeed pronouncing these words for the first time, and, unlike a courtesan or a débauchée, she intends them as true. But Flaubert's novelistic universe is precisely one in which there is no possible distinction between "sincere" language and "empty metaphors." To complain of the inevitable triteness of language is to imply that the soul whose "fullness" words fail to express is not itself as trite as the words themselves. While this is no doubt a legitimate position, it can hardly be said to be the one that Flaubert has been taking throughout the novel; it is certainly not that of the Fair scene.

Yet if we read Flaubert's words as mere self-expression, reflecting a momentary transformation of the impersonal author into an opinionated narrator, we are missing the point. As an intervention of the *author,* they constitute a complaint about the language not merely in, but of, his novel, about the impossibility of creating an original fictional universe when man is condemned to the endless repetition of clichés without definable origins. If there is truly no way of distinguishing between the original and unoriginal use of words, then it would be futile to attempt to write a novel essentially different from *Madame Bovary,* to attempt to create Selves rather than Others. The author's lament is as much a commentary on his own labors as on the limitations of Rodolphe's judgment.

Nonetheless, we cannot ignore "the dissimilarity of feelings" that Flaubert here attributes to Emma. In speaking to Rodolphe she is indeed expressing the "fullness of her soul" because she believes, however naively, in the power of language to express the authenticity of her emotions. By declaring without reserve her submission to her lover, she is not uttering hollow phrases, but defining herself by an act of faith. In this, Emma achieves a genuine albeit second-level superiority to the other characters in the novel. The forms of her action are not original, but she alone believes that these forms can be lived in the real world, that these "empty metaphors" can be filled out with life. It is not only Rodolphe but the reader who can be reproached with not seeing Emma's superiority. Her naivety lies in her belief that the bourgeois world must recognize the superior value of the person who puts its romantic rhetoric into practice, whereas it has created this rhetoric precisely in order to avoid having to deal with the question of *real* differences in value. If everyone can find words to express his or her own uniqueness, then it is no longer necessary to engage in humiliating competitions to find out who is really unique. Flaubert was the first novelist to discover this truth, a discovery which, as this passage shows, is not without its frustrations.

Flaubert's lament is of particular interest because it reveals a new complicity with Emma, whom he defends not only as a true heroine but as his personal representative in the world of the novel. The concluding reflection on language was not present in Flaubert's earlier drafts of this scene; it appears to constitute an irruption of the author's self-consciousness into the fictional world of his creation. When Flaubert began *Madame Bovary,* he intended to describe a world organized around the desires of someone unlike himself. But here we discover that the Self-as-Other is not a part of the world the artist rejects, but his ally against it. If Emma cannot rise above clichés, neither can Flaubert himself, the difference being that in his authorial role Flaubert need not live by them. The author alone is in a position to comment on the unoriginality of language without thereby demonstrating his own unoriginality.

Flaubert was not the first writer to reveal that the language of worldly desire can never fulfill its promises. But unlike his romantic predecessors, he expresses this revelation not in a "higher" language from which these illusions are excluded, but in the very words of this deluded desire. In this editorial comment on his characters and their language, the author allows his heroine to share for a moment in his originality, something she has no way of doing within the world of the narrative.

EMMA AT THE OPERA (CHAPTER 15)

Emma wants Rodolphe to run away from Yonville with her; instead, he leaves town without her, cynically justifying his action in a letter filled with romantic verbiage. Emma falls into a deep depression. To distract her, at Homais's suggestion Charles takes Emma to Rouen to see the celebrated tenor Lagardy in Donizetti's opera *Lucia di Lammermoor*. It is here that she will renew her acquaintance with Léon, who will become her second lover.

The following passage is situated immediately before the reappearance of Léon. Emma is wholly absorbed in the spectacle:

> [Lucia is about to be married against her will] Ah! if only, in the freshness of her beauty, before the defilements of marriage and the disillusion of adultery, she could have entrusted her life to some great solid heart, then with virtue, tenderness, sensual pleasure and duty all united, she would never have had to descend from such a height of felicity. But that happiness, no doubt, was a lie imagined to make one despair of all desire. She now knew the pettiness of the passions that art exaggerated. Making an effort to turn her thoughts away from it, Emma wanted to see in this reproduction of her sufferings nothing more than a vivid fantasy good only to please the eyes. . . .
>
> [Lucia's lover Edgar, played by the famous Lagardy, suddenly appears.] He must have an inexhaustible love, she thought, in order to be able to pour it out on the crowd in such broad waves. All her notions of disparagement melted away beneath the poetry of the role that invaded her, and, drawn to the man by the illusion of the character, she tried to imagine his life, that spectacular, extraordinary, splendid life, and yet a life she might have led, if chance had willed it. They would have met, they would have loved! With him,

through all the kingdoms of Europe, she would have traveled from capital to capital, sharing his fatigue and his triumph, picking up the flowers thrown to him, herself embroidering his costumes. . . . But a mad idea seized her: he was looking at her, for certain! She wanted to throw herself into his arms to find refuge in his force, as if in the incarnation of love itself. . . .

This is Emma's first serious contact with art since her girlhood in the convent. In the first paragraph, she momentarily attains an illusory wisdom that is swept away in the second by the appearance of the leading tenor.

This passage is an excellent example of Flaubert's use of free indirect discourse. The first sentence of the first paragraph is clearly a reproduction of Emma's thoughts. As we have observed, the absence of narrative commentary on these thoughts empties them of truth-value; they are neither true nor false, merely the expression of a hypothesis concerning her existence that could never be tested. If only she had found the "great solid heart" she sought . . . but in the world of free indirect discourse, such hearts by definition cannot exist. The following sentence calls this imagined happiness a lie; Emma appears to have acquired sufficient experience of the world to reject her first, self-indulgent fancy. In the third sentence, "she knew" makes an apparent transition between subjective and objective narration; the next sentence will speak of Emma in the third person.

But the status of this knowledge is problematic. If Emma really "knew" the pettiness of passions, then her relapse into illusion in the following paragraph would be incomprehensible. If this is true, then the sentence beginning "She knew" should be read as a continuation of the free indirect discourse that precedes; yet there is no objective mark in the text that tells us this. The characteristic ambiguity of free indirect discourse is reflected in the ambiguity of the "knowledge" that is available to Emma; in discourse without a subject, no statement of objective knowledge is possible. Even the wisest observation can only be a subjective impression of knowledge, another form of worldly illusion. Whether Emma really knows that romantic love is a sham cannot be tested so long as she remains within the world of the novel.

Emma's realization that ideal happiness is a lie is at most a momentary intuition without practical consequences. Lacking any other set of categories with which to understand the world, Emma cannot abandon her illusions. Yet this fleeting intrusion of truth is a sign of progress. Emma has exercised her judgment in rejecting her first, more naive impression. Within the subjective language of free indirect discourse, the beginnings of a process of liberation are revealed. But in *Madame Bovary* this can only mean liberation *from* the world, not in it. Emma's awareness of the lie of passion is in fact her first step toward suicide.

For now, Emma remains in the world. In the following paragraph, with Lagardy's appearance on stage, she is swept back into the utopia of her dreams. Where the first paragraph expresses a movement toward objectivity by changing from free indirect discourse to the third person, the second makes this transition in reverse. At first, "she thought," then "she tried to imagine"; but once her imagination has caught on, free indirect discourse is used in the rest of the passage.

The key to the contrast between Emma's attitudes in these two paragraphs is the different imaginary models they contain. The figure of Lucia di Lammermoor, although it generates at first an image of romantic bliss, is no longer sufficient to hold Emma's attention; the hope for a "great heart" strikes her as illusory because she has only the models of the men she has known to fill out the image. But she can no longer reject the dream once she is in the presence of a figure who stands apart from her own world. What attracts her to Lagardy is less the role of Edgar he is playing than the man himself, with whom she sees herself touring the great capitals, embroidering his costumes, and hearing him sing for her alone. What Emma had rejected in the preceding passage was the "lie" by which art "exaggerated petty passions." Now it is not Lucia's passions that she imagines as fulfilled, but her own desire for worldly success and recognition. The "great heart" she had despaired of finding now appears realized in the "force" in which she wants to take refuge.

Lagardy, like the Viscount of the Vaubyessard ball, acts as a catalyst for the beginning of a new extramarital love affair. But whereas the Viscount was a member of a traditionally privileged social group, Lagardy is an artist who stands outside mundane social categories. Emma swiftly extrapolates from his role in the opera to the life that makes this man "the very incarnation of love." This attachment to the artist, as opposed to the specific illusions of art, constitutes the final stage in Emma's quest for fulfillment. In the first, her youthful readings generate the image of a Prince Charming that prepares her for marriage. In the second, she becomes disillusioned with her life with Charles, but finds in her brief experience of the Vaubyessard ball the source of a new, more concrete illusion that leads to her affair with Rodolphe (for whom she has made a cigar-case identical to the Viscount's). Now, disillusioned with worldly lovers of the kind that Lucia is awaiting in the opera, she puts her faith in the artist's transcendence of all specific social roles.

Throughout the novel, Emma has shown signs of a George Sand-like adoption of masculine modes, wearing men's clothes, smoking in public, wearing her hair in male fashion. The relationship with Léon is marked by a more fundamental role reversal. In Emma's final vision, the ideal lover has become the artist; but when this dream is translated into a real love affair, it is Emma rather than Léon who will play the artist's part. (As a curious sign of Emma's transformation, this part of the novel contains reminiscences of Flaubert's youthful work "Les Baladins" whose protagonist, a female street performer, commits suicide in the grand romantic manner. Emma's walk to the hotel where the lovers meet takes her past the Rouen theater district; one night she even dances in a masked ball.) Rodolphe was a vulgar substitute for the Viscount, a reasonably dashing member of the gentry, a representative of the aristocratic sexual and social freedom Emma could obtain only vicariously. But the dream of the artist's life transcends both the purely literary models of her girlhood and the worldly ones that the ball had provided her. The Lagardy she dreams of is an extension of his role on the stage. The source of the strength she attributes to him is her imagination, not his; her desire for this strength is more an identification than a mere passive yearning. Thus in her final liaison, rather than merely inciting her lover to fulfill her ideal of masculinity, Emma will play the leading role in creating a world of shared illusion. If Lagardy's performance as an operatic lover makes him appear to Emma as the "incarnation of love," it is Emma who will appear to Léon as "the lover of all the novels, the heroine of all the dramas."

13

Part 3

THE AFFAIR WITH LÉON

The following passages reflect the evolution of Emma's relationship with Léon, from its idyllic beginnings to inevitable disillusionment.

1. The Idyll (Chapter 5)

The warm apartment, with its discreet carpet, its fanciful ornaments and its quiet lighting, seemed perfectly suited to the intimacies of passion. . . .

. . . They were so completely lost in the possession of each other that they believed they were there in their own home, and that they were to live there until death, like two eternal newlyweds. . . .

[Léon] was savoring for the first time the inexpressible delicacy of feminine elegance. Never had he encountered this grace of language, this reserve in dress, these poses of a languid dove. He admired the exaltation of her soul and the lace of her petticoat. Besides, wasn't she *a woman of the world,* and a married woman! in a word, a real mistress?

By the diversity of her moods, by turns mystical or joyous, chatty, taciturn, emotional, passionate, nonchalant, she would call up in him a thousand desires, awakening instincts or reminiscences. She was the lover of all the novels, the heroine of all the dramas, the vague *she* of all the volumes of poetry. . . .

Often, as he looked at her, it seemed to him that his soul, fleeing toward her, spread out like a wave on the contour of her head, and was drawn down into the whiteness of her bosom.

2. Disenchantment (Chapter 6)

. . . in the letters that Emma sent him, she wrote of flowers, poetry, the moon and the stars, naive resources of a weakened passion, which tried to revitalize itself with any and all external aids. She would continually promise herself, for her next trip, a profound happiness; then she would admit that she had felt nothing extraordinary. This disappointment was soon wiped out by a new hope, and Emma returned to him more inflamed, more avid. She would undress brutally, ripping off the thin lace of her corset, which hissed around her hips like a gliding snake. . . . and pale, without speaking, serious, she would fall upon his chest, with a long shudder.

They knew each other too well to have those moments of wonder in possession that multiply its joy a hundredfold. She was as sick of him as he was tired of her. Emma was rediscovering in adultery all the platitudes of marriage. . . .
She continued nonetheless to write him love letters. . . .
But in writing, she perceived another man, a phantom made of her most ardent memories, of her most beautiful readings, of her most powerful cravings; and in the end he became so real, and accessible, that she quivered with wonder, yet without being able to imagine him clearly, so hidden was he, like a god, under the abundance of his attributes.

The first passage describes the early phase of Emma's affair with Léon, during their Thursday meetings in a Rouen hotel. The scene is described mostly from Léon's point of view. It is Emma whom we see arriving and leaving the hotel, but once inside "their" room, Léon's perspective predominates. It is sometimes even expressed through free indirect discourse, a form that is generally reserved for Emma.

The couple's happiness is described without irony; what reference there is to its illusory nature refers to their notion that they could remain "eternal newlyweds" indefinitely. Emma no longer associates amorous satisfaction with hopes for the future; she savors these moments with the avidity of someone who realizes that time is running out. No longer does she dream of beginning life anew, as she had hoped to do with Rodolphe. It is rather Léon who dreams, while Emma absorbs herself in creating for him the image of a perfect love. But while Emma clearly plays for him the dominant figure of the "older woman," their idyllic moments, in contrast to Emma's previous experience with Rodolphe, are times of reciprocity rather than submission. Emma's superiority as the architect of their relationship compensates for the passivity of the woman's role. She no longer seeks to be consumed by male desire, but to arouse it and take pleasure from it. This is indeed a utopian moment in the novel. But the modern reader should avoid reading it anachronistically as the depiction of a model love relationship. Emma's dominance comes at a price; her "artistic" role in sustaining the idyll requires continual injections of capital. Both sexually and financially, Emma, having exhausted the value accumulated through her adolescent mortifications, is living beyond her means. She becomes increasingly extravagant, sells some family property without Charles's knowledge, and is rapidly depleting her financial resources.

Emma's sensuality becomes more intense as she feels her capacity to become absorbed in it slipping away. Emma is experiencing no longer the failure but the death of illusions. Her attempts to make herself believe in the permanence of the relationship merely signify that she believes in it less and less. The "platitudes of marriage" that she finds in adultery signal the end of even physical pleasure, the descent into ultimate boredom. It is no coincidence that this last stage corresponds to financial ruin. As the goods she buys give her less and less satisfaction, she is obliged to spend more and more, like a drug addict whose habit grows increasingly expensive as it becomes less pleasurable. Emma is living on borrowed time with borrowed funds.

Flaubert's world contains no real producers, only consumers. But for Emma in this period consumption becomes an increasingly creative enterprise. She fashions herself into an aesthetic figure for Léon's benefit, and becomes in her love letters an active rather than a passive user of romantic language. Although she seeks to create illusion rather than to denounce it, she experiences despite herself something of the writer's detachment from her creation. In the very effort of writing she exhausts her capacity for desire; as the author puts it, "these movements of vague love tired her more than great debauches." Emma has reached the stage where she must write her own novels in order to be able to continue to believe in the imagery she had once accepted from without. The same is true of the lies she is continually obliged to tell Charles to hide the real reason for her trips to Rouen; her life has become a continual creation of fictional discourses intended to cover up an increasingly unsatisfactory reality. Thus Emma becomes a kind of "novelist," but this only makes the difference between her and the author more apparent. For her creativity is limited by the necessity of living in the world, and eventually, by that of dying in it.

It is the third part of the novel that most upset the readers who wanted to condemn Flaubert for obscenity. Emma's aggressive sensuality unmasks the reader's pretensions at masculinity along with those of Léon, who had become, in the author's words, "more her mistress than she was his." The Other's desire, which has throughout the novel been defined by her passive acceptance of cultural clichés, takes on a life of its own in her despairing attempt to impose these clichés by force on the real world.

"What does a woman want?" Flaubert's answer at first seemed unthreatening: a woman wants what we have told her to want. In order to keep herself pure for marriage, she must be taught to believe that her sacrifice of present pleasures will be rewarded by the arrival of a "heavenly lover" who will introduce her to unsuspected joys. In taking up with Rodolphe, Emma is still paying homage to this dream, having decided that adultery rather than marriage is the true locus of romance. Now, in her final state of disillusionment, she no longer hopes to find an ideal lover ready-made, but tries to transform her real lover into her ideal. By now the literary and cultural sources of this ideal are beside the point. Emma desires to be possessed by a man whose worldly existence she knows to be impossible.

Even on a superficial level, this is an emasculating experience for the man who can never live up to her impossible expectations. But there is a deeper significance to this situation, which Léon experiences in terror as "the absorption, greater each day, of his personality." The Other appears as bottomless pit, a black hole. It is not enough to say that the masculine Self is humiliated because he is unable to satisfy his partner's emotional and sexual desires. The Self is a finite being whose identity depends on his maintaining a separating distance between himself and his objects of desire. But the Self-as-Other has no such limitations. Existing only through the force of the Self's desire, the Other has no stake in maintaining this separation. The Other's ultimate fulfillment is the complete absorption of the Self, the breakdown of all difference that is its death as a differentiated being.

This understanding of the Other is not limited to the sexual sphere, with its obvious figures of female interiority and male exteriority. The object of desire always appears at the center of a circle, with the self on the circumference, attracted by the central object but maintaining an existence independent of it, an existence which is in fact dependent on the object's inaccessibility. But if this "object" too desires, then how is this distance to be maintained? The cult of the beloved that reaches its high point in the High Middle Ages with the *Divine Comedy* has sometimes been explained through association with the adoration of the Virgin, who had not originally been a major figure in Christian theology. But these cultural phenomena are reactions to an uncomfortable relationship with otherness rather than its cause. Man does not put woman on a pedestal as a sign of his mastery over her. The reality of the situation is quite the reverse: he exalts her far above his desire in order to avoid the uncomfortable situation of having to face her own.

The sexual inequality thus maintained is not so much a form of exploitation as it is a protective device that enables the modern self to be born. But since the Other is really only another Self, no amount of cultural manipulation can do more than postpone the ultimate confrontation between the two. Flaubert was able to face the question of the Other's desire in *Madame Bovary* because he saw the evolution of bourgeois society as leading not to the Other's accession to selfhood but to the extension of otherness to the Self. In this development, woman rather than man provided the critical model. His heroine is less a figure of oppressed womanhood than an archetype of the human being in the modern world.

We have seen that Emma's desires originate in her readings and religious experiences. Throughout the evolution of bourgeois society, woman has been the consumer par excellence of cultural products. During the eighteenth and nineteenth centuries, and even to some extent today, the reader of novels is presumed to be female—men being supposedly too involved in public activities to engage in such frivolous pursuits. The basis of this phenomenon is not simply that women of the cultivated classes have generally had more leisure time than men. As cultural Others, destined for the role of object rather than subject of desire, women were the privileged recipients of culture. When Emma learns to identify her adolescent sexual "sacrifices" with the forms of religious observance, we may say that she is being "socialized" to her role as an object for male desire. She is being taught to exalt her value as a desire-object to a point at which she will not be tempted to engage in the give and take of the mutual search for sexual pleasure. With the breakdown of the pattern of socialization described in *Madame Bovary,* this kind of exchange, forbidden to respectable middle-class women in Flaubert's time, has become characteristic of contemporary sexual mores.

If woman had always been the special object of culture, Flaubert understood that in modern society subject and object have become essentially equivalent. We become involved with Emma not through pity for her condition, but because we sense that her Otherness reveals the real truth of our so-called Selfhood. As the victim of culturally fostered illusions, Emma is the bad conscience of modern society. The terror that she comes to inspire in Léon reflects the fact that modern man faces, in his Other, his double. The liberation of the energy that had heretofore been bound up in romantic dreams is a threat to a social order that in Flaubert's day still depended on essential human differences, beginning with the difference between the sexes. If Emma were merely debauched, if she merely sought sexual pleasure to satisfy physical appetites, her character would be far less disquieting. But by confronting her lover with the infinite, quasi-sacred images of romantic desire, Emma challenges him to an infinite expense of energy, the Herculean effort of trying to fulfill man's own cultural ideals.

In the affair with Rodolphe, things never got out of hand because Emma was passively following her models, reading into Rodolphe's tawdry reality the wondrous hopes she had at first associated with her marriage. But now the situation is reversed. As Emma increases her efforts to assimilate Léon to the man of her dreams, his own role is continuously diminished. If we see Léon as a prototype of the ordinary modern bourgeois unredeemed by art whom Flaubert reviled, then Emma is the image of this man's desire for selfhood and significance thrown back at him, the incarnation of his empty illusions about "meaning in life." He is unable to turn away from her, not out of mere sexual dependency, but because he cannot fail to recognize that his very being is dependent on the impossible desire that she feels not so much for him as *about* him. *Madame Bovary* suggests that in the modern world, to be human is not so much to desire as to be desired, to find one's place in the marketplace of interpersonal exchange.

EMMA'S DEATH (CHAPTER 8)

It has been noted that Emma's final downfall is due less to her amorous disappointments than to her financial irresponsibility. The merchant Lheureux (the French means "the happy one") has exploited her penchant for luxury, cynically aware of her sexual irregularities. Emma's destruction is carried out in the "hard" marketplace for goods rather than in the "soft" one of personal relations because only in the former can the unreality of her position be objectively demonstrated. Although she has indeed exhausted the sexual capital accumulated during adolescence, she has learned as an "artist" to create new values of this kind. Even had Léon left her to marry and settle down, as he does shortly after her death, disillusions in love would most likely have augmented rather than diminished Emma's sexual attractiveness. But the inadequacy of her creativity in the intimate sphere is revealed by her financial insolvency. Her active role in organizing—and financing—the idylls with Léon drives Emma to live ever further beyond her means.

In the prototype of consumer society that Lheureux prophetically creates for Emma, romantic discourse, like that of advertising, is never confronted with the truth, but it is nonetheless made the basis of the practical action of consumption. Just as Emma tries to realize romantic dreams of love in a bourgeois world, so she attempts to recreate the decor that surrounded the heroines of her novels. But her dealings with Lheureux show that she has misunderstood or "misread" the discourse of modernity. The point of advertising is to get you to buy, perhaps even on credit, but the experienced consumer is expected to realize that one can never have everything advertising makes one want. Emma, for whom consumer society is a personal rather than a public reality, is incapable of manifesting this bourgeois self-restraint.

Rather than her increasingly tyrannical personal impositions on him, it is Emma's financial demands that bring about Léon's departure. As soon as she asks him for three thousand francs to pay a part of her debts, the objective values of the marketplace take over and Léon is liberated from his dependency. Returning to Yonville after failing to obtain anything from Léon, Emma visits various admirers in unsuccessful attempts to obtain the money she needs. The local *notaire* (an estate lawyer, who often acted as a private banker and investment counselor) seems ready to offer her the sum in exchange for her favors, but she has not yet sunk low enough to accept this degree of prostitution. Finally she goes to Rodolphe, but he cannot or will not help her. Now all seems to fall apart, and Emma resolves on suicide:

This decision is prepared by a striking passage:

> [Emma] remained lost in a stupor, conscious of herself only through the beating of her arteries, which she imagined she heard escaping from her like a deafening music that filled the countryside. The earth beneath her feet was softer than water, and the furrows

seemed to her immense brown waves breaking. All her mind's contents of memories, of ideas, escaped at once, in a single explosion, like a thousand pieces of fireworks. She saw her father, Lheureux' office, their room back there [in Rouen?], another landscape. Madness was taking hold of her, she became afraid, and was able to pull herself together, in a confused manner, to be sure; for she did not recall the cause of her horrible state, that is, the question of money. She suffered only in her love, and felt her soul escape from her through this memory. . . .

It seemed to her all at once that fire-colored balls were exploding in the air like incendiary bullets flattening out, and they were spinning, spinning, then falling to melt in the snow, among the branches of the trees. In the center of each, Rodolphe's face appeared. They multiplied, and they came nearer, penetrating her; everything disappeared. She recognized the lights of the houses, which glowed far off through the fog.

Then her situation, like an abyss, presented itself.

Readers have been struck by the similarity of this scene to Flaubert's own descriptions of his quasi-epileptic fits. The contents of Emma's memory appear to escape from her like fireworks or exploding bullets. This is a form of hallucination, but quite the opposite of what is usually meant by that term. Instead of being confronted by products of her imagination imposing themselves on her from without, Emma feels them deserting her mind to go elsewhere; rather than an excess, her hallucination takes the form of a loss. Unlike the victim of ordinary hallucinations, who is unaware that the visions that terrify him have their source in his own imagination, Emma is frightened by her inability to hold on to what she had thought of as her unique personal memories.

This peculiarly Flaubertian type of hallucination deserves more than a medical interpretation. Whatever type of nervous disease her creator may have had, for Emma this experience serves as a cure for the romantic imagination that has dominated her life since adolescence. The experience of hallucination as loss brings about in her a heightened lucidity. The terrible truth this loss reveals is that these thoughts and memories were never really her own. A parallel can surely be drawn with the 1844 attack that led to Flaubert's affirmation of his vocation as a writer. For Flaubert too, the long-term lesson of this hallucinatory loss was that the imaginary desires he had called his own were really an impersonal cultural acquisition. Flaubert's "realism" is nothing more than his lucid obedience to this lesson, which required him to resist the romantic temptation to attribute a higher truth to the products of his desiring imagination.

Emma next experiences a series of apparently random memories (of her father, Lheureux, the hotel room). Each succeeding image is vaguer and less personal than the preceding one; each also appears in a more distant perspective (note the "back there" associated with the image of the room in Rouen). These memories concern the different forms of security that men have brought to her life. Her father, the only figure who appears in person, had once provided this security by his very presence. Lheureux' office, which she has just left, is the place where her doom was sealed; but throughout the vicissitudes of her love affairs, Lheureux has furnished the luxury items that made up the all-important decor of these adventures. The security the merchant provided was illusory, but at least the articles were real. In contrast, the memory of "their bedroom back there" alludes to her trysts with Léon, but it is the empty locus of an illusory paradise. The final item, "another landscape," is defined only by its otherness, the "somewhere else" where she hoped to find the elusive amorous satisfaction of which she dreamed, to which her imaginary lover was to carry her off.

The vagueness of "another landscape" offers no security, not even that of four walls, nor is there an imaginary lover to occupy it. Its emptiness is a sign of alienation, and Emma draws herself up in terror. But Emma has forgotten that her desperate situation is caused by imminent financial ruin rather than by disappointment in love. She has lost sight of the beginning of the series; she recalls, so to speak, the movement of exile from the room to the landscape, but not the more fundamental alienation represented by Lheureux. The merchant is the real, unbearable symbol of Emma's love life. Her mistake had been to take consumer's satisfaction as a model for amorous satisfaction; to regard the availability of the luxury goods that provided the setting for her desire as a guarantee that the desire itself could be fulfilled.

Finally her imagination becomes concentrated on Rodolphe, who

121

has just rejected her plea for money. Her visions spin around her, even "penetrate" her, in a movement that parodies the dizzy spinning of the ballroom in her dance with the Viscount at the Vaubyessard ball. Instead of representing a train of thought, these images are all identical; there is only a single object of desire that stands for all the others. This image is as it were her last chance of salvation; just as Emma's last attempt to raise money was directed at Rodolphe, so is the final effort of her imagination. This, after all, was a concrete experience of love and sexuality, not just a dream or an inadequate episode of conventional reality like her marriage.

With the images of Rodolphe, "all disappears"; Emma has fired the last round of her desiring imagination. In what Flaubert describes as a "transport of heroism" she decides to end her life by taking the arsenic she knew to be available in Homais's pharmacy. Emma has joined the lucid suicidal heroines of his youthful romantic works.

Once Emma has taken the poison she experiences a sudden calm, as though "in the serenity of an accomplished duty." At this point, her progression from living cliché to exemplary figure is complete. The acceptance of death is the renouncement of the search for worldly fulfillment. Authentic life requires the metaphoric death-in-life of the dedicated artist, for which Flaubert himself provided a model. But the heroine of his novel does not have the option of dying metaphorically. Her suicide is a condemnation of the world from within, a demonstration of life's meaninglessness that at the same time gives her fictional life its cultural meaning.

On her deathbed, Emma expresses affection for her husband and recognition of his goodness, as well as relief at the end of her life of desire. The scene of extreme unction created something of a scandal: as the priest anoints the different parts of her body, Flaubert describes "her eyes, which had so coveted all earthly luxuries . . . her mouth, which had opened for lies, which had groaned in pride and cried out in sensuality. . . ." As pointed out in the defense brief at the trial, these words do not reflect an original conception but one adapted from ecclesiastical tradition (and one used not many years previously in a well-known novel by the writer and critic Sainte-Beuve). This emphasis on the religious element is not mere faithfulness to social reality. At the moment of her death, the religious imagery and ritual in which Emma had sought guarantees of future worldly satisfactions become meaningful in themselves. The passionate kiss she plants on the crucifix, described as "the greatest kiss of love she had ever given," functions in the opposite manner from her youthful devotions: instead of converting religious values into the capital of imaginary sensuous satisfaction, it expresses the religious nature of her quest for absolute love.

But it would be too simple for Emma to end her life on this serene note of return to tradition, as though the eleventh-hour consolations of religion provided a genuine reconciliation between desire and reality. Just after taking the sacrament, at the very moment of her death, there appears outside the window a grotesque blind man that Flaubert created solely for the purpose of making him present at this scene. Emma had first seen the blind man on the route home from her trysts in Rouen, where he sings the first verse of a little song that makes an ironic commentary on her loves. Now he sings the song to the end:

All of a sudden, there was heard on the sidewalk a noise of heavy wooden shoes, with the scraping of a stick; and a voice rose up, a hoarse voice, singing:
> Often the warmth of a sunny day
> Makes a young girl dream of love.

Emma started up like a galvanized corpse, her hair undone, her pupils fixed, gaping.
> To gather up diligently
> The ears of grain that the scythe reaps
> My Nanette goes bending toward
> The furrow that gives them to us.

—The blind man! she cried.

And Emma began to laugh, with an atrocious, frantic, desperate laugh, thinking she saw the hideous face of the wretch, who rose up in the eternal darkness like a figure of horror.
> It blew very hard that day,
> And the short skirt flew away!

A convulsion threw her back upon the mattress. Everyone approached. She had ceased to exist.

The hideous blind man is a refugee from the romantic grotesqueries of Victor Hugo who seems out of place in the sober setting of Flaubert's novel. His song is an ambiguously sinister statement of the parallel between love and death of the kind typical in the late Middle Ages. Nanette's leaning toward the furrow carries a suggestion of both sexual availability and mortality; the song sketches the relationship between procreation and death, sowing and harvesting, from a pagan rather than a Christian perspective. Yet this is a "paganism" very familiar to the Christian world, one which its loftiest visions of redemption were never able to suppress. Nor is its lesson about love and mortality lost on Emma.

The blind man's function in this scene is obvious—perhaps too obvious. However authentic a kiss she gave the crucifix, Emma is both too small and too great to end her life in the bosom of a church represented by poor Bournisien. Too small, because her deathbed liberation is the result not of the acceptance but of the refusal of life. (Flaubert never takes up the question of the suicide Emma's right to a Christian burial, preferring to let us assume that the local priest believed Homais's tale that her poisoning was accidental.) But above all, she is too great, too much of a sacred figure in her own right. Emma's suicide, like those in the author's youthful works, is a condemnation of the world for its inadequacy to her desires. The grotesque blind man expresses the ambivalence of the heroine's romanticism, which is at once a form of uncomprehending mimicry and the expression of a higher wisdom than that of bourgeois society. Emma's violent reaction to his interruption of the deathbed ceremony shatters the prevailing ritual calm. Her "atrocious, frantic, desperate laugh" is both the Byronic-Satanic sneer of a superior being without illusions and a pathetic cry for help. However exaggerated we may find this episode, it is not unfitting that a living ghost from the romantic past should become the object of Emma's final thought. She had failed to find in the bourgeois world an incarnation of the romantic lover of her novels, but she was at least able to encounter a genuine figure of romantic horror.

The blind man has a significant counterpart in Flaubert's later work. In "Saint Julian the Hospitaler," published in 1876 and included in his *Three Tales*, Flaubert tells the story of a medieval nobleman given to violence who, after mistakenly killing his parents in a fit of rage, serves penance as a boatman ferrying passengers across a wide river. One day a leper covered with sores asks Julian not only to ferry him across but to let him warm himself at his fire, then to lie down in bed with him to let him obtain the warmth of Julian's body. Although the leper is a hideous creature, Julian obeys, and the leper is transformed into Christ and carries him off to paradise.

The blind man of *Madame Bovary,* unlike the leper, is a grotesque figure who elicits little sympathy from either the author or his characters. Yet the resemblance is genuine. Both are outcasts who express the material horror of our mortal condition too directly for civilized society to tolerate. To accept this figure is to acquire in the Flaubertian universe a dignity analogous to that of the artist, who must acquiesce in the world as it is without judging it. Julian's sainthood, like Saint Anthony's vision of fusion with matter, is a model of Flaubert's own aspirations.

Because Emma has experienced the humiliation of the Other's role, she cannot remain indifferent to this figure of otherness. Her reaction to him is not, like Julian's, a gesture of redemption; it is closer to a sign of damnation. But it conveys to us something of the romantic sense of the superiority of lucid Satanism to superficial salvation. The blind man is that which cannot be assimilated by the bourgeois mentality, that which only the artist has the courage to face. Homais, the novel's chief incarnation of this mentality, will have the beggar put away in an institution after promising and failing to cure his skin disease. Emma lacks the strength to embrace this figure, but she is lucid enough to recognize in him a kindred spirit; for her existence has been, like his, a refutation of bourgeois society's pretension of having exorcised the horror of the human condition.

Bibliographic Essay

Editions of *Madame Bovary*

French

The standard French text of *Madame Bovary* is contained in the Conard edition of Flaubert's complete works (1910–54). A more accessible scholarly edition, with an introduction and a good set of notes, is that of the Classiques Garnier (Paris: Garnier, 1971) edited by Claudine Gothot-Mersch. This edition unfortunately no longer contains the trial briefs. A number of pocket editions of *Madame Bovary* are available, notably those of Livre de Poche and Garnier-Flammarion, both of which do include the trial materials.

Flaubert's writing was marked by an extraordinary number of alterations and suppressions. A "new version" of *Madame Bovary* that uses the original manuscripts to reconstruct a kind of "first draft" of the novel is Jean Pommier and Gabrielle Leleu's *Madame Bovary: Nouvelle version* (Paris: Corti, 1949). Examination of this work, which also contains Flaubert's detailed plot outlines for the novel, is indispensable for the scholar who wants to get something of the flavor of Flaubert's rigorous methods of composition. This compilation is based on manuscripts published by Mlle Leleu in *"Madame Bovary": Ebauches et fragments inédits* (Paris: Conard, 1936).

English Translations

The first extant English translation of *Madame Bovary,* still reprinted by the Modern Library (New York: Random House) as late as 1950, was completed in 1886 by Eleanor Marx-Aveling, Karl Marx's daughter, who, like Emma, took her own life. This remains a fine translation, often more faithful to the nuances of Flaubert's style than those that have followed it. However, its language is outdated, and it does not follow the modern practice of reproducing the original paragraph divisions. This translation has recently been reprinted (without attribution) in a low-priced edition by Airmont Books.

A version of the Marx-Aveling translation modernized by Paul de Man is used in the Norton Critical Edition of the novel (New York: Norton, 1965). The book contains excerpts from Flaubert's drafts and plans, as well as a rich selection of critical texts including the historic articles by Sainte-Beuve and Baudelaire. Much of this material does not exist elsewhere in English. This fine translation and useful reference work is rather more expensive than other paperback editions and more difficult to find in bookstores. The bibliography, over twenty years old, should be updated.

The best-known American translation of *Madame Bovary* is that of Francis Steegmuller, which replaced Marx-Aveling's in the Modern Library in 1957. It is a reasonably faithful rendering, although it often puts grace of expression ahead of adherence to the original text. Steegmuller has taken particular care to reproduce Flaubert's imperfects, a difficult task in English.

Mildred Marmur's Signet Classic translation (New York: New American Library, 1964) is one of the more reasonably priced versions available in bookstores. It is on much the same level of accuracy as Steegmuller's, and in small details misconstrues the French text. The book includes the transcript of the trial.

Alan Russell's 1950 translation, published by Penguin Books (Middlesex, England, and Baltimore, Md.), is the most elegantly written of the group. It is considerably less accurate than the previous two, paying little attention to verb tenses or even paragraph divisions. Its redeeming feature is Russell's sensitivity to the effects of Flaubert's style, for which he is often uncannily successful at finding English-language equivalents.

Bantam Books (New York) has recently reprinted Lowell Bair's

1959 translation in its "Classic" series. This reasonably priced edition features an introduction by Professor Leo Bersani, a selection of critical essays by writers from Zola to Sartre, and a bibliography. The translation is sensitive to stylistic nuance, accurate in details, and overall the most faithful of the lot.

Although none of these translations comes as close to Flaubert's own prose as today's reader might like, all are satisfactory. The Norton edition, the most expensive, has the best critical apparatus and a good translation. The Bantam translation is a notch ahead of the others, and its inclusion of critical texts makes it an excellent choice. Both Steegmuller's and, in a different way, Russell's translations are also worthy of recommendation.

Other Works by Flaubert

French

There are three major editions of Flaubert's complete works:

The Conard *Oeuvres complètes de Gustave Flaubert* (Paris: Conard, 1910–54, 26 volumes, including 13 volumes of *Correspondance*) remains the standard, although it is scarcely a critical edition by modern standards.

The Edition du Centenaire (Paris: Librairie de France, 1921–24, 14 volumes) and the *Oeuvres complètes illustrées de Gustave Flaubert* published by the Club de l'Honnête Homme (Paris, 1971–75, 16 volumes) improve the critical apparatus and include a few additional texts.

A convenient and inexpensive two-volume edition of Flaubert's complete works is that of the *Collection Intégrale* (Paris: Éditions du Seuil, 1964), edited by Bernard Masson. This contains everything in the Conard edition but the *Correspondance,* including the juvenilia and travel notes, the first *Éducation sentimentale,* and the three versions of the *Tentation de Saint Antoine.*

Of the more readily available editions, the Classiques Garnier (all the major works) contain extensive notes and variants; inexpensive editions are available from Livre de Poche and Garnier-Flammarion.

Two volumes of Jean Bruneau's exhaustively annotated (and unexpurgated) edition of the *Correspondance* have appeared (Paris: Gallimard, Bibliothèque de la Pléiade, 1973 and 1980), covering the period up to 1858. For the later years, the (expurgated) Conard edition must still be used.

English Translations

There is no modern English edition of Flaubert's complete works, although all his novels and a number of the youthful works are readily available in English. Penguin has included translations of all the major works in its Penguin Classics series.

A recent two-volume selection of the *Correspondance*, based in part on Bruneau's new edition, has been translated by Francis Steegmuller (Cambridge, Mass.: Harvard University Press, 1980–82).

Critical Studies of *Madame Bovary* (French)

Of the numerous critical studies in French, one of special interest to readers of *Madame Bovary* is Claudine Gothot-Mersch's *La Genèse de Madame Bovary* (Paris: Corti, 1966), which corrects a number of previously held inaccuracies concerning the origins and sources of the novel. Albert Thibaudet's *Gustave Flaubert,* originally published in 1922, and recently reprinted in a popular edition (Paris: Gallimard, Collection Tel, 1982), remains the most perceptive study in any language of Flaubert's style and technique.

Bibliography

Primary Works

Titles with an asterisk (*) were published posthumously. Dates given are the first publication by Flaubert or, for posthumous publications, of completion.

Juvenilia, 1835–39*
Mémoires d'un fou, 1838*
Novembre, 1842*
(First) *L'Éducation sentimentale,* 1845*
Par les champs et par les grèves, 1847*
La Tentation de Saint Antoine (first version), 1849*
Notes de voyage (Middle East), 1849–50*
La Tentation de Saint Antoine (second version), 1856*
Madame Bovary, 1857
Salammbô, 1862
L'Éducation sentimentale, 1869
Preface to Louis Bouilhet's *Dernières chansons,* 1872
Le Candidat (drama), 1874
La Tentation de Saint Antoine (third version), 1874
Trois contes, 1877
Le Château des coeurs (féerie), 1880
Bouvard et Pécuchet, 1881*
Correspondance, 1830–80*

Secondary Works

Books on Flaubert in French

Bollème, Geneviève. *La Leçon de Flaubert*. Paris: Julliard, 1964. Establishes the relevance of Flaubert's doctrines to the narrative techniques of the *nouveau roman*.

Bruneau, Jean. *Les Débuts littéraires de Gustave Flaubert (1830–1845)*. Paris: Armand Colin, 1962. Contains unpublished texts and much valuable information on Flaubert's youth.

Debray-Genette, Raymonde, et al. *Travail de Flaubert*. Paris: le Seuil, 1983. Includes a number of important essays on *Madame Bovary* by major critics, notably Jean Starobinski and Claude Duchet.

Dumesnil, René. *"Madame Bovary" de Gustave Flaubert*. Paris: SFELT (Les Grands Evénements Littéraires), 1946; original edition, Paris: Edgar Malfère, 1928. Discusses the composition and publication of the novel; by the leading *Flaubertiste* of the first half of the century.

Proust, Marcel. "A propos du 'style' de Flaubert." In *Contre Sainte-Beuve*. Paris: Gallimard, 1971. A justly celebrated 1920 essay on Flaubert's stylistic technique.

Richard, Jean-Pierre. "La Création de la forme chez Flaubert." In *Littérature et sensation*. Paris: le Seuil, 1954. Important essay on Flaubert's literary perception.

Rousset, Jean. "*Madame Bovary* ou le livre sur rien." In *Forme et signification*. Paris: José Corti, 1962. Major "structuralist" study of the novel.

Books on Flaubert in English

Barnes, Hazel. *Sartre and Flaubert*. Chicago: University of Chicago Press, 1981. A study of Sartre's *The Family Idiot*, including an analysis of *Madame Bovary*, by a distinguished American Sartrean.

Barnes, Julian. *Flaubert's Parrot*. New York: Knopf, 1985. Ostensibly a novel, but really a wistful and whimsical essay on the elusiveness of the "real" Flaubert.

Bart, Benjamin F. *Flaubert*. Syracuse, N.Y.: Syracuse University Press, 1966. The most thorough literary biography, by the dean of American Flaubert studies.

Bart, Benjamin F., editor. *"Madame Bovary" and the Critics: A Collection of Essays*. New York: New York University Press, 1966. A useful collection of historical (Pater, James) and academic studies.

Brombert, Victor. *The Novels of Flaubert: A Study of Themes and Techniques*. Princeton, N.J.: Princeton University Press, 1966. Elegantly written analysis in a traditional mode.

Bibliography

Buck, Stratton. *Gustave Flaubert.* New York: Twayne, 1966. Useful short literary biography.

Culler, Jonathan. *Flaubert: The Uses of Uncertainty.* Ithaca, N.Y.: Cornell University Press, 1974, 1985 (paperback). Radical but judicious postmodernist study of Flaubert's "uncertain" narrator.

Fairlie, Alison. *Flaubert: Madame Bovary.* London: Arnold, 1962. Stylistically sensitive in-depth reading of the novel.

Gans, Eric. *The Discovery of Illusion: Flaubert's Early Works 1835–1837.* Berkeley: University of California Press, 1971. Young Gustave's assimilation and rejection of romantic literary modes.

Ginsburg, Michal Peled. *Flaubert Writing: A Study in Narrative Strategies.* Stanford, Ca.: Stanford University Press, 1986. Highly perceptive deconstructionist study, best on the early works and *Madame Bovary.*

Giraud, Raymond, ed. *Flaubert: A Collection of Critical Essays.* Englewood Cliffs, N.J.: Prentice-Hall, 1964. Useful collection of studies by critics of the last generation.

Haig, Stirling. *Flaubert and the Gift of Speech: Dialogue and Discourse in Four "Modern" Novels.* Cambridge: Cambridge University Press, 1986. Discusses free indirect discourse and other aspects of Flaubert's use of language.

LaCapra, Dominick. *"Madame Bovary" on Trial.* Ithaca, N.Y.: Cornell University Press, 1982. Analysis of the novel's deconstructive effect on its time.

Sartre, Jean-Paul. *The Family Idiot.* Translated by Carol Cosman. Chicago: University of Chicago Press, 1981–87. Volumes 1-2. The first two volumes of Sartre's monumental three-volume sociopsychological study of Flaubert, dealing mostly with his youth. Brilliant and provocative, but verbose and not always reliable.

Sherrington, R. J. *Three Novels by Flaubert: A Study of Techniques.* Oxford: Oxford University Press, 1970. Solid, sensible studies of the major novels.

Shor, Naomi, and Henry F. Majewski, editors. *Flaubert and Postmodernism.* Lincoln: University of Nebraska Press, 1984. Flaubert as seen by the deconstructive generation.

Spencer, Philip. *Flaubert, A Biography.* London: Faber & Faber, 1952. Still an excellent biography.

Starkie, Enid. *Flaubert: The Making of the Master.* London: Weidenfeld and Nicolson, 1967. Insightful but regrettably careless; the frontispiece photograph of Flaubert is actually that of his friend Bouilhet!

Steegmuller, Francis. *Flaubert and Madame Bovary: A Double Portrait.* Chicago: University of Chicago Press, 1939, 1950, 1968, 1977 (paperback). A historical semi-fiction in the old style, but full of psychological finesse.

Thorlby, Anthony. *Gustave Flaubert and the Art of Realism.* New Haven, Conn.: Yale University Press, 1957. Perceptive study of Flaubert's novelistic technique.

Vargas Llosa, Mario. *The Perpetual Orgy: Flaubert and Madame Bovary.*

Translated by Helen Lane. New York: Farrar Straus Giroux, 1986; original Spanish edition, 1975. A personal essay full of provocative historical and psychological insights.

Other Relevant Works (English Translations)

Auerbach, Erich. *Mimesis*. Translated by Willard Trask. Princeton, N.J.: Princeton University Press, 1968. This classic study of the literary depiction of reality contains an analysis of a scene from *Madame Bovary*.

Girard, René. *Deceit, Desire and the Novel*. Translated by Yvonne Freccero. Baltimore: Johns Hopkins University Press, 1965. Includes *Madame Bovary* in its pantheon of novels that reveal the truth of "metaphysical desire."

Poulet, Georges. *Metamorphoses of the Circle*. Translated by Carley Dawson et al. Baltimore: Johns Hopkins University Press, 1967. Includes a celebrated analysis of Emma's "circular" experience of marital boredom.

Index

Index

About the Author

Eric Gans was born in New York City in 1941. He attended Columbia University (B.A. 1960) and received his doctorate in Romance Languages from the Johns Hopkins University in 1966. He is currently professor of French at the University of California, Los Angeles, where he has taught since 1969. Among his books are *The Origin of Language* (1981), *The End of Culture: Toward a Generative Anthropology* (1985), and *The Discovery of Illusion* (1971), a study of the early works of Flaubert. He has also published several books in French.

Dr. Gans's principal field of specialization is nineteenth-century French literature. Over the last decade, he has elaborated a theory of "generative anthropology" that attempts to explain the phenomena of language and culture on the basis of a hypothesis of human origin as a unique event. His other professional activities are translation and microcomputer programming.